I, Juan de Pareja

Elizabeth Borton de Treviño

• • • •

With
Connected Readings

PRENTICE HALL
Upper Saddle River, New Jersey
Needham, Massachusetts
Glenview, Illinois

ISBN 0-13-437496-7

3 4 5 6 7 8 9 10   03 02 01

PRENTICE HALL

Acknowledgments

Grateful acknowledgment is made to the following for permission to reprint copyrighted material:

Curtis Brown, Ltd.
The Boy Who Drew Sheep by Anne Rockwell, first published by Atheneum. Copyright © 1973 by Anne Rockwell. From "A Time of Beginnings" in *No Chinese Stranger* by Jade Snow Wong. Copyright © 1975 by Jade Snow Wong.

Farrar, Straus & Giroux, Inc.
I, Juan de Pareja by Elizabeth Borton de Treviño. Copyright © 1965 and copyright renewed © 1993 Elizabeth Borton de Treviño. All rights reserved. Published by arrangement with Farrar, Straus & Giroux, Inc. "Large Bad Picture" from *The Complete Poems 1927–1979* by Elizabeth Bishop. Copyright © 1979, 1983 by Alice Helen Methfessel. Reprinted by permission of Farrar, Straus & Giroux, Inc.

Greenfield Review Press
"Stone Carving in Kotzebue" by Jim Schoppert. First appeared in *The Greenfield Review*. Reprinted by permission of the Greenfield Review Press, Greenfield Center, NY.

Harvard University Press
"The Angle of a Landscape—", #375 from *The Poems of Emily Dickinson*, Thomas H. Johnson, editor, Cambridge, Mass: The Belknap Press of Harvard University Press. Copyright © 1951, 1955, 1979, 1983 by the President and Fellows of Harvard College. Used by permission of Harvard University Press.

Alfred A. Knopf, Inc.
From *My Name Is Asher Lev* by Chaim Potok. Copyright © 1972 by Chaim Potok. Reprinted by permission of Alfred A. Knopf, Inc.

(Acknowledgments continue on p. 160.)

Contents

I, Juan de Pareja

I, Juan de Pareja

Elizabeth Borton de Treviño

Foreword

THE first half of the seventeenth century was brilliant with names that still shine with the luster of courage, art, science, and glory. It was the age of Shakespeare's maturity, the age of Richelieu, Sir Walter Raleigh, and of Cervantes' *Don Quijote*. It was the age of Descartes and Spinoza, the age of the first Romanov tsars and of St. Vincent de Paul. Rembrandt, Rubens and Van Dyke were painting in the Low Countries; Galileo, Newton and Harvey were contributing scientific knowledge that would turn conceptions of the material world into new channels. Corneille, Racine, and Molière were writing in France. Louis XIV was to come to the throne in France, and in Spain the court painter was Diego Rodríguez de Silva y Velázquez. By his side, handing him brushes and grinding his colors, was a Negro slave, Juan de Pareja.

Against this background of a Europe yeasty with new ideas and with burgeoning power and art, I have chosen to tell the story of a simple slave.

Slavery had been a commonplace in Spain since the advent of the Moorish conquerors, for the Arabs had always dealt in African flesh. Europe of that day seemed to have no idea that slavery was wrong; it had developed from a Greece whose democratic ideal was based on a foundation of slave labor. Even the ancient Hebrews, who awakened our conscience, had slaves. There are, alas, many countries in the world which still buy and sell slaves, but it is typical of our age that we reject this great evil and insist upon the dignity and freedom of all men, clumsy though we may be in some of our attempts to achieve these ideals.

My story deals with Juan de Pareja, and with Velázquez, his master.

One

In which I learn my letters

I, JUAN DE PAREJA, was born into slavery early in the seventeenth century. I am not certain of the year. My mother, who was called Zulema, was a very beautiful black woman, and though she never told me who my father was, I suspect that he was the keeper of one of our master's warehouses, a white Spaniard who could not afford to buy her. But I know that he did give her a golden bracelet and gold hoops for her ears.

She died when I was about five, and I was not told any more than that she had flown away to heaven. I have always wondered what happened. Perhaps my life might have been different if she had survived. It is likely that she died of a fever or some other illness. Seville, where we lived, was seldom without fear of the plague, for so many ships from foreign ports sailed up the Guadalquivir to tie at our docks, and anyone who died of a mysterious malady was hastily buried, in fear and trembling and in the hope that he had not brought us the pest.

I missed my mother terribly, for she had always rocked me to sleep in her arms, even when I was a large child, and she sang to me softly in her deep rich contralto. Even now that I am an old man, and have come through so much, I can close my eyes and hear her voice humming the songs I loved, feel her arms around me, warm save for the pressure of her golden bracelet, and enjoy for a fleeting moment that sense of safety and of love with which she surrounded me.

She was a tender creature, lavish with small caresses and kindnesses. When she sat sewing on the mistress's garments, in the light of an eastern window in the early morning, she pierced the silks and velvets gently with her needle and smoothed the stuff with her slender, sensitive dark hands. Looking up at me, she would smile, and her melting eyes would send love toward me, like a touch.

Ay, my mother. I have some knowledge of painting now, hard gained over the years of my life, and what a challenge to a painter you would have been! What a delight and a torment to try to catch the soft sheen of apple green taffeta and garnet velvet of the mistress's gown, the sober brown of yours, the pink and gold of your turban, picked up by the gold hoops in your ears and the beautiful dark glow, like that of a ripe purple grape, along your round cheek and slender neck. And how to paint your lovely hands, fluttering over the silks like two dark birds?

After my mother's death, the mistress took me for her page boy and dressed me in a fine suit of brilliant blue silk, and set an orange and silver turban on my head. Also, she gave me my mother's earrings, though she kept the bracelet and wore it. Mistress pierced my ear herself and drew a thread through the hole, moving it a bit each day until it healed, and then she hung one of the hoops in my ear.

"It cleans the blood to wear an earring," she told me. "There! I shall keep the other one for you, in case you lose this."

Mistress was kind but capricious, and she was often forgetful because she adored Master so much and he was always ailing, a constant worry to her. Mistress was a de Silva, of Portuguese descent, from the city of Oporto. It was my duty to walk behind her when she went out to the shops or to take sherbet with her friends, carrying her reticule, her fan, her missal, her rosary in its little pearl-studded box. "Juanico," she called me. "Juanico, my fan! No, do not hand it to me, fan me with it! I am suffocating with the heat. No, no, not so hard, you will muss my hair!"

I soon learned, with the fatalism of slave children, not to be surprised when she slapped me with her closed fan, a sharp rap that sent sudden pain along my hand and made tears sting under my eyelids. Just as suddenly, she might turn and set my turban straight and pinch my cheek fondly. I was in the same category as her little tan-and-white dog, Toto, which she alternately cuffed and cuddled.

Yet I was devoted to Mistress. When I was sick she watched over me and got up in the night to bring me broth. She saw that I had clean water to wash in, and she gave me a piece of her own soap each time she ordered the long white bars for her bath. She fed me well and saw that I had money to buy sweets in the street, and sometimes she let me go to watch the strolling players or to the fair.

I will always be grateful to her for one thing—she taught me my letters. My mistress, I realize now, like many women of her class, had very little education. She read slowly and laboriously, and it always took her several tearful afternoons to compose a letter to her family in Portugal or to her nephew in Madrid, a young man who was a painter. Yet Mistress had a great deal of practical wisdom, and she knew many things because she trusted her judgment and cultivated her memory.

One hot afternoon in September she called me to her bedroom, and for once she did not begin immediately to list a series of errands and duties for me to perform. She was wearing a gauzy cool dress for, although she had drawn the curtains to keep out the sun and to preserve the colors of her Moorish carpet, the room was warm and her forehead was damp. She was fanning herself, gasping a little.

"Stand over there, Juanico," she said. "I wish to study you." She took a long, steady look at me. Then she nodded her head. "Yes," she said to herself. "Yes, I believe he is intelligent enough. Quite."

Then she spoke to me, mopping her neck with a large white cotton handkerchief.

"I am going to teach you the alphabet," she told me. "If you pay attention and practice well, you will learn to write a fair hand, and then you will be able to do my letters for me, and perhaps later on help Master at the warehouse. I will arrange that nobody is to bother you while I am having my afternoon siesta; in those hours you are to practice."

I was not very old at the time, nine perhaps, and the thought of learning something that provoked as much anguish as it seemed to cause the mistress when she sat down to write a letter, did not attract me. But I knew how impetuous she was, how changeable. I merely answered, "Yes, Mistress." I was certain she would forget all about it.

But she did not, even though a thunderstorm came up in the night and rain poured, refreshing the city and washing away the dust. For the next day dawned cool and bright, the kind of weather when she loved to promenade and show off her fine clothes, made from the rich materials her husband brought from Turkey and Persia.

The morning started as usual. When she called me, she was attired in a robe of plum color and was wearing gold chains around her neck and her black lace mantilla. We swept off to Mass, I walking just a step behind her, carrying her sweetmeat box, her rosary, and a little switch with feather tufts, to be used for frightening away mangy dogs or dirty street urchins who might press too close.

Mass was in the great cathedral, with its soaring arches, its tall pillars, its glinting gold on altars and picture frames, its soft candlelight in the scented gloom. This was for me, as always, a delight. I loved the melodious chanting of the priests, the beauty of their vestments, the glorious moment of the elevation. Mistress often had to rap me with her fan in church, for I quite forgot her, her sweetmeats and her rosary, everything, while I sent my soul upward to bathe in a golden light which seemed to come down from God.

After Mass I hoped Mistress might go to the house of a friend who sometimes made that strange American drink for us, foaming chocolate, and served it hot in tiny cups. Mistress always allowed me to finish the last sips in her cup. I loved it and tried to keep the sweet taste on my tongue for minutes afterward. But this day Mistress took the short way home and rustled along ahead of me almost in a hurry. She went straight to her room and it was one of the serving maids (a country girl with thick wrists and ankles who was saving up her wages to get married) who got the sharp edge of Mistress's tongue for not having made the bed and aired the room.

"Get about it and have everything in order in ten minutes," ordered Mistress, "for I wish to work at my desk and I cannot bear to see a tumbled bed."

Mistress put away her Mass veil and rosary and rolled up her sleeves above the wrists. Then she set out her ink pot and quill, and I saw that she had not forgotten her threat to teach me to make my letters.

We began at once with A and we went through B and C and D that very morning. I learned from Mistress what sound each letter represented, and it came to me with a flash of joy that in learning to write I would also learn to read. So, later, when Mistress had her nap, I applied myself to my task and practiced carefully, for Master had a library with many leather-bound books in it, and he spent hours there, enchanted, reading aloud and laughing to himself and shouting and making comments on what happened inside the book covers. I longed to learn what his books told him that gave him so much pleasure.

Master was a dark, slender man with a skin that had gone yellow from so many fevers. He was always sickly. He had warehouses and counting rooms down on the wharves, and he went there early every morning. He could not abide breakfast. "My liver cannot work until I have had a brisk walk," he would tell Mistress when, in one of her imperious moods, she commanded him to have breakfast. She liked very much to eat, and periodically she insisted that he take a coddled egg or a morsel of fish poached in wine, or some other tidbit. Usually Master came back to the house about three in the afternoon to eat his frugal meal, and then Mistress would have rages of love and frustration, for he would not taste the dainty dishes she herself prepared for him, asking only for boiled vegetables and a crisp crust of bread.

"But you eat like a monk!" Mistress used to rail at him, though he seldom answered her, but only smiled and patted her hand to calm her. After resting, he always went into his library where he passed such happy hours, quite alone.

Envying him his books, I worked hard at my writing, and for once Mistress was consistent and steady. Every day, no matter what else was planned, she checked my bit of rag or Damascus paper, and gave me new letters to draw. When I began to make them better than she, she was annoyed at first, but after a little, her common sense came to her rescue and she cried, "There, I knew it! Juanico, I declare, you will write a good hand that no one could be ashamed of. Your letters are round and clear, and you draw the tails on them most beautifully! You like doing this, no?"

I hung my head so that she could not see how much I loved it, for she was capricious, and if she thought I preferred doing the letters to anything else, she might make me do other things for a while, to keep me humble.

So time went by, and eventually I began to write all her letters. Especially when Master was ill and she was very busy with him, bathing him, and attending him in every way she knew, she would often make me sit with pen and paper while she distractedly dictated, the while changing the water on cut flowers, or airing the sickroom, or measuring out Master's medicine. "Write to my sister in Oporto, Juanico—you know the address— and tell her that we are about the same here. My darling husband eats almost nothing, even broth will not stay on his stomach, and he has terrible pains." Dashing away her tears with the back of her hand, she would continue, "Ask her to send me two big skins of the very best Oporto wine, and also some of the herb we used to take as tea when we had upset stomachs when we were children . . . she will remember the name of it. Tell her to send me the wine and the tea by the very first messenger, and I will reward him when he arrives. And send my love, and say at the end all the things I always say in my letters. Do this one right away and bring it to me today."

Sometimes I drew little designs on the borders of the letters, to illustrate some point. Perhaps a bit of lace from a handkerchief, or a small bird, an orange, or the mistress's little dog Toto. She was amused by these and did not scold me for them.

Master became more and more ill. At last he could not leave his bed and our house was very sad. I remember now the letter Mistress had me write to her nephew in Madrid, after Master's death.

My dear Diego, I have to give you most sorrowful news. You
know how your Uncle Basilio always loved you. Now he will
never embrace you again. He was in such pain in the last
months that I dare not weep, for it was God's mercy that
gave him peace, and I must be grateful to Him. But I am
lonely and in the dark now, for my dear companion is beside me no more. He was much older than I, and he spoiled
me, but I loved him very much. *Ay de mi.* I hope to make the
journey to Madrid to visit you, as you have so often invited
me, but I will pass my first year's mourning here in Seville.
Your uncle planted a little orange tree in a tub, a new kind,
very sweet and juicy. I shall bring it to you as a gift from
him when I come.

Your loving aunt,

Emilia.

From this letter I knew that we would be in Madrid in a year's
time, and I began to think very much about Don Diego, the
nephew. I learned from remarks here and there that he was a
painter of great talent, but taciturn, severe, and strange. I
thought it would be wonderful to watch him work, and I hoped
there would be such moments when I was not occupied with
duties toward Mistress.

I knew that Don Diego had been a pupil of Pacheco and had
married that great painter's daughter. I determined somehow
that I would one day worm my way, under some pretext, into
Pacheco's studio, for he was still working in Seville and had
many pupils. How I would love to visit a painter's studio, watch
him lay on the colors, see the visions of his trained eye appear,
little by little, on the clean white canvas!

But Mistress kept me close at home, for she never went out
now except to Mass. She was fretful and became thin from fast-
ing and from tears, and sometimes it was all I could do to bring
a faint smile to her lips. Toto and I tried our best to divert her.
She was busy, too, going over accounts at the warehouse,
though the long columns of figures made her head ache.

But I managed to get near Pacheco's house on a day in summer. It turned out to be a sad day; I shall never forget it. That
day portended much trouble and suffering for me, but I did not
know it when I skipped out into the fresh early morning before
the sun was high, to bring fresh bread from the baker's. I ran,
taking the long way round, hoping that as I passed the painter's
house I might catch a glimpse of him working inside his patio,

for this was the hour when maids washed down the doorsteps and threw buckets of water into the streets to lay the dust, and the big *zaguán* was wide open.

As I came near I saw that a funeral cortege was forming; horses stood draped in black net, tossing black plumes on their heads. A coffin was being carried out of Pacheco's house. I questioned some boys near by and I learned that the painter's youngest daughter had died in the night and they were now taking her to church to be present at her last Mass before burial.

"There's pest in the city," they told me, crossing themselves. "And there are funerals all over. It came in with a boatload of slaves and ivory from Africa. Listen! The death bells are tolling!"

I listened to the solemn dirge of many church bells. In my haste I had not heard them, for the sound of church bells was always in our ears and had become something of which I was not conscious.

Frightened, I ran away to the bakehouse, but there the doors were barred shut and a big sign of the cross, still wet with paint, glistened in the morning sunlight and told me that someone within was dying of the plague.

Then I rushed home, breathless with fear that I might find our own door locked and the terrifying advice drawn on it with hasty strokes. In this I was prophetic, or intuitive; call it what you will, I have often had these flashes of news in advance of their happening. Because the very next morning it was I who, with tears streaming, painted the cross on our *zaguán*, and before that day was gone Mistress was being prepared for burial.

When she was taken away, to the tolling of sad bells, I could not follow, for I had fallen sick most suddenly and was past all thinking. I lay on my cot dreaming of water and burning with fever, suffering dreadful hallucinations and terrors, drenching sweats, horrible retchings and vomiting. I have no idea how many days and nights I lay thus at the point of death.

When at last I came to my senses, rose, and weakly went in search of food, I found that there were no servants, and there were dust and silence everywhere. I had been abandoned.

I drank water from a half-filled wooden bucket, and in the patio there were a few oranges on the trees. I was too feeble to climb for the best ones, but I ate one that had fallen to the ground, all overripe as it was. I was ravenously hungry.

Afterward I slept again, deeply and without dreams. A tremendous pounding on our front gate woke me finally, and though I was still weak, I managed to make my way, reeling, along the corridors and call out, "*Quién?* Who is there?"

It was a friar in a worn, brown robe, one of those I had often seen in the streets of Seville, going about caring for the sick and dying. He came in and washed me and made me a fresh bed and tucked me into it, and he cooked hot broth and fed it to me with a wooden spoon.

"I'm Brother Isidro," he told me, "and it is God's miracle that you are alive, boy. Every other soul that was in this house has been laid in earth." He paused to cross himself and murmur a prayer.

He was an old man, with a fringe of white hair, and he had lost several teeth, so that his words whistled unexpectedly. At one of those whistles, we heard a little sound, half yelp, half moan, and Brother Isidro went bustling about to see where it came from. He discovered Toto, all thin and starving, his pretty coat stiff with dirt. The poor little dog must have hidden in the house all those days. Brother Isidro clucked to him and then he fed him broth, too. Toto licked his hand and then crawled toward me.

"Poor little fellow," murmured the friar. "I will take him with me; they will care for him at the convent. And you, boy, you must pray and give thanks, and ask to be shown why God has chosen to save you. There is something He wants you to do; there is some duty He has laid upon you."

"What duty?" I whispered.

"He will tell you in His own good time," answered Brother Isidro. "He will show you what you must do and why He has kept you in this life. Just as He showed me. I was a soldier, going out to the Indies, when my ship foundered and went down with all hands, and only I was saved. I found a spar and clung to it until I was rescued. But while I was washing about in the sea, I saw in a dream that I was meant to nurse the sick, and I have been doing it ever since.

"Now I will come back tomorrow morning to look after you and bring you food, and you must lie and sleep and rest and pray. We will see what is to become of you and where you are to stay."

"I am a slave," I told him. "I am Juan de Pareja. I belonged to Doña Emilia de Silva y Rodríguez."

"I will make inquiries. And I will care for this little dog. Now do not get up; you are still weak and might take a chill."

He hurried about, washing up his bowls and spoons and stowing them into a big leather sack he carried. Heaving this up on his shoulder, he picked up the little dog and pattered away. I heard the great front door closing behind him.

I tried to pray, but I did not say more than a few words before sleep overcame me.

I learned from Brother Isidro a few days later that I had been inherited, along with all the other property, by the painter in Madrid, Don Diego Rodríguez de Silva y Velázquez.

Two

In which I prepare for a journey

BROTHER ISIDRO was followed into the house next day by a magistrate, a tall, severe, middle-aged gentleman dressed in black velvet, who wore a heavy gold chain around his neck from which hung an imposing medal. Behind him came a slave boy about my own age, who carried an inkpot and quill, and who rolled his eyes fearfully at every step as if he was terrified of stumbling and spilling the precious black India ink, and by a spindle-legged clerk who struggled along under the weight of a great leather-bound book into which the magistrate presently began to write his lists. First, though, he tested several chairs before choosing one to sit upon; then he had a small table brought to him and the great book laid upon it.

"Bobo, you may put the inkpot down. There. When I tell you, you may dip the quill into the ink. Not yet! I haven't arranged my thoughts, decided upon procedure."

Brother Isidro, bowing humbly, said, "Please, your worship, would you not note down the boy Juanico here, and let me take him away to the convent, to strengthen him for his journey?"

The magistrate looked at Brother Isidro very sternly.

"When I am ready to note down the name and description of this slave, I shall do so, and not before," he announced. "Meanwhile, let him make himself useful bringing out the books from the library. Each one must be described and checked against the list in the will of the late Don Basilio Rodríguez, may he rest in peace."

"Could not . . ." began the little friar once more, but he was silenced with a look and with a hand held up imperiously.

So, staggering still with weakness, I began bringing out the books, armloads of them, and it took all the morning for the magistrate to check them against his lists. Brother Isidro, with many things to do, had gone about his business with only a promise to return for me, and by the time the cathedral bells were marking noon, I longed for the sight of his little red, wrinkled, kindly face as I had never longed for Master.

The magistrate at last sighed, shook sand over the pages in his book, and closed it. He rose to his feet and strode toward the door, followed by his clerk and his slave. The *zaguán* clanged shut after them and I found my way, tottering and exhausted, back to my cot.

But Brother Isidro came for me toward dusk, bringing me bread and cheese. He also had a cloak for me, some castoff that a rich lady had tossed him for his poor charges. I was glad to wrap it around my shivering shoulders, though the day was warm.

"You will stay in our convent; Brother Superior has given his consent," the friar told me, "and we will not let them take you away until you are well. I know the magistrate and his kind. They mean no harm, they are not actively cruel, but they simply do not see. They look at a black boy and they see only a slave who is capable of doing work. They do not see what I do."

I was stumbling along behind him as he hurried on his sandaled feet through the narrow streets of Seville.

"What do you see?"

He slowed down a little as he sought words to answer me.

"Well, I see a person. A boy. A human being with a soul, made in God's image," he told me. "Have you made your first Communion?"

"Oh yes," I answered proudly. "Mistress saw to that. And I used to go to Mass with her. Every day." At the thought that I would never see her again, or Master, or the house which had been my home, I started to cry. I felt the big tears rolling down my cheeks. Brother Isidro turned, as he heard me sniffling, and patted me awkwardly.

"Now, now," he said. "Let us repeat our Rosary as we walk, and that will comfort you. Poor child. We must go a good piece still, for the convent is outside the city. Better for you, as I shall not let the magistrate know for a week or so where you are. I can be very deaf when I need. God forgive me for this bit of deceit. I won't lie; I shall simply keep out of his way. Hail Mary, full of grace. . . ." And so, saying the prayers as we jogged along, the dear familiar words did soothe me and get me over the rough stones and the ruts in the road until Brother Isidro tugged at the rope hanging down outside the monastery gate.

There was much confusion within, a great running to and fro of assorted children, lame and sick people, old persons, animals. Toto came running to me, and I stooped down to pet him, feeling the little bones close under his hide. But he had been washed, and his small belly was distended with food.

This place was not at all my idea of conventual life, which I had thought of as ordered, silent, and comfortable. But I soon learned that this convent was different from most, being a kind of asylum. Besides, the brothers were very poor, and what little they were given they spent prodigally on the forgotten, the sick and the abandoned of the city—any suffering creature, human or animal. I might have realized, had I stopped to analyze matters, that I, a sickly and useless slave, could not have been of much use to one of the wealthy convents dedicated to scholarship, to copying and decorating manuscripts, and to intensive prayer before the Blessed Sacrament. In our Father's house are many mansions, I remembered, and each has special duties.

Brother Isidro, scolding all the horde of children, old men and women on crutches, little galled donkeys and flea-bitten dogs which pressed against him, called out irritably for help, and several other friars, as poorly clad as he, came to relieve him of his big sack of bread.

"Now make lines, do not push," called Brother Isidro. "There's enough for all, blessed be God." The crowd somehow got itself thinned out and into order. I had managed to stay by his side, so I was allowed to help him. We broke the bread into chunks, and another brother held out to each pitiful derelict, a little wooden bowl full of broth. Into this the bread was sopped and crumbled, and all ate. The animals were given dry bread and there were a few bones for the dogs.

Brother Isidro and I ate later, in his cell, while another friar passed out sacks and covers and found places for all to sleep.

"We do what we can," he told me, blessing his crust and giving thanks. "We keep them for a few days and beg for them. God is good, and usually our sacks are full when we come back from asking alms in the city. We pass the little children on to be apprenticed, wherever we can find places for them. The old and crippled we keep on to help us. They help us beg, of course, and some of them we send out never come back. A few *maravedis* in their hands, a piece of bread. . . . Well, we will not judge. We do what we can," he said again, biting off a piece of his coarse black loaf.

"I wish I could stay with you forever!" I cried out.

"I wish you could. But you are to be sent to Madrid." I shivered.

"It is a fair place," the friar told me, "and if you keep your heart soft and your soul clean, you can find good to do. There is much to be done in this wicked world."

"I am only a slave . . . a servant," I complained, feeling sorry for myself.

"Who is not?" asked Brother Isidro, briskly. "Do not we all serve? In any case, we should. That is nothing to be ashamed of; it is our duty."

I slept that night on his cot, which was of wood and had no

cover. But I had the cloak he had given me, and in the morning he came to wake me and bring me bread and a slab of cheese.

"Stay here today and make yourself useful," he told me. "The Superior says that you are to look after the little ones. And save your strength; you must be strong for your journey."

I did not remember that last remark of his until later when I was on my way to Madrid with the gypsy muleteer.

In the meantime, I spent six busy days in the convent. There were perhaps twenty friars, Franciscans all, who were trying to live in holy poverty, sharing with the needy. Busy as I was, sponging feverish little ones with cool cloths, helping the cripples to get about, persuading the querulous old ones to eat their crusts and to walk about in the sunshine instead of huddling in the dark, I began to send my thoughts forward to Madrid and to my new master.

Every night I waited for Brother Isidro with great impatience. Sometimes he had two great sacks, full of turnips or onions or other farm produce. Always he had bread, bought at a bake oven with the coins he collected as alms during the day. I watched his face avidly for news, and then it came. The next day we were to go back into the city; I was being sent north.

This time I enjoyed the walk along the dusty road. I loved the smell of the dry grasses and the sound of the crickets which arose in clouds before us. I sang as we went.

We came to Seville and began to walk along narrow, stone-paved streets. It was a part of the city I did not know.

"The house where you lived has been sold," Brother Isidro told me. "I am taking you to the home of the magistrate."

At a big heavy door of wood studded with bronze knobs, Brother Isidro stopped and took the knocker (a curious one, in the shape of a fish) in his hand, and banged it three times. The door swung open and we stepped into a wide hall that seemed unusually dark because of the brilliance of sunshine in the inner patio, where a fountain sparkled and sang.

We were made to wait in the hall. At last a manservant came to lead us to the office of the magistrate, who transacted his business affairs in a quiet room toward the rear.

He sat at a long carved table with his papers strewn about and his fingers all ink-stained. He did not rise, but waved Brother Isidro to a seat and curtly directed me to stand outside in the corridor. I could not hear what they were saying, but Brother Isidro emerged looking both angry and sad. He put his arm around my shoulder and then he blessed me, so that I knew I should not see him again. My heart constricted at this new parting, and I could not answer. Brother Isidro hurried away and I was left to await orders. I let my wild unhappy imagination run away with me as the hours dragged by and no one came to tell me what to do or where to go. And I was too timid to ask. In the convent I had been ill and weak at first, but with duties, with a personality and responsibility. Now I was well, but once more a cipher—not a person but a slave.

I don't know how much time went by. Servants came and went, brushing past me as if I were invisible. Visitors were ushered into the magistrate's office, sat and murmured, and came out again. My feet and legs grew tired from standing, but there was no place to sit. When I could bear it no longer I slumped down and sat on the floor, my back to the wall. And there, with my head lolling, I fell asleep.

I was awakened some time later with a sharp kick in the leg. I don't suppose the fellow meant to hurt me, really, but the ignominy of it, the fact that I had fallen asleep in such a disrespectful position, my sudden conviction of being adrift and lonely, all upset me, and made me cry. At my first sob I received another kick, one meant to startle me into silence. I gulped and scrambled to my feet.

The man standing over me was a house servant, wearing dark cotton clothes and a big green apron; brushes and cleaning rags protruded from his pockets.

"Come along with me. The Master will give you your orders."

I overcame my first nervousness and went along sullenly.

I was taken, not into the office where I had seen Brother Isidro enter, but into the magistrate's bedroom. He had removed the black jacket of his suit and was wearing only tight knee-length black trousers, shoes and stockings, and a fine white cotton shirt, ruffled in front.

"Now what is your name?" asked the magistrate, in an irritated tone. "I haven't my papers with me."

"I am Juan de Pareja," I told him.

"Yes, Juanico. Well, you may go to the kitchen and have something to eat. You can sleep in the stables tonight. Tomorrow morning early you are to go out with all the goods of Doña Emilia to her nephew Don Diego, in Madrid. On the way, I trust you will earn your keep by helping the muleteer; I was awarded no moneys to feed you, either here or on the way. But I am," he sighed, "a merciful man and I will not send you away hungry."

Now I had lived long enough and had heard enough from

urchins my age and from other slaves, to distrust the person who calls himself merciful, or just, or kindly. Usually these are the most cruel, niggardly and selfish people, and slaves learn to fear the master who prefaces his remarks with tributes to his own virtues.

I felt chilled, and when, in the kitchen, the cook handed me a dirty bowl of lukewarm soup, and nothing else, I felt a premonition of trouble.

Looking about me, I observed that the kitchen was a poor one. There were no strings of onions and peppers hanging across the ceilings; there were no hams and sausages on hooks. And there were locks on the sugar and flour bins. The cook was thin and bad-tempered, and I realized that the magistrate was probably something of a miser. "A light in the street and darkness at home," went the Spanish saying, and he was one of those who moved with dignity and decorum in public, but lived in penury and discomfort inside his fine shell of a house.

The stables at least were a bit better maintained than his kitchen. There were several fine, well-fed horses. The harness was shiny and supple with oil, and the brass decorations were brilliant. No one came to show me where I might lie, so I made a bed for myself atop a heap of straw and covered myself with one of the blankets used to throw over the horses when they were brought in sweating from a hard journey.

Three

In which I meet Don Carmelo

BEFORE dawn I was awakened by having a cup of cold water flung in my face, and grinning down at me I saw faintly in the light of the fading stars, a dark, scarred face. The man seemed to be about thirty or so; he was broad-shouldered and handsome in a savage way, with fine teeth and large flashing dark eyes. I soon made out from his clothes and from the orders he was shouting that he was the muleteer who was to lead us to Madrid. I got up in a hurry and offered to make myself useful to him.

He was a Romany, lithe and graceful, strong as a panther, quick in his movements. I carried water and fodder and helped load the mules, and I was made most respectful of the touchy animals, especially one which tried to bite me and then danced itself around to be in a position to kick me. But I had learned something of mules when Don Basilio sold his goods at the warehouses, since merchants usually took their purchases away on muleback, and I was able to protect myself. The gypsy, when he saw me in trouble, walked over and calmly struck the mule a heavy blow on the nose, and even though I was glad to be safe from flying hooves and sharp teeth, I pitied the poor beast, for blood gushed from his nostrils and he hung his head as if stunned.

"You'll get the same, little blackamoor, if you make any trouble," said the gypsy, with a brilliant smile. I soon learned that that bright smile was a warning; the gypsy loved to subdue anything and make it subservient to him. I was not a rebellious child, though often a sullen one, and I soon learned to leap to obey Don Carmelo. That was his name. Carmelo, really. Only gentlemen have the right to use the Don. But he insisted that I address him as Don. I noticed that the magistrate, when he came out to give final orders, spoke to "Carmelo."

There were ten mules in all, and we went heavily burdened, for Don Carmelo did not spare them. I wondered how far he would make us go in a day's march, and I feared the worst. But I need not have worried about that. Don Carmelo loved to sing and dance and to drink wine, and he gave himself plenty of time at each evening stop so that he might enjoy himself to the fullest wherever there was a gypsy camp. So, though we were sorely loaded, we were not pressed too far. It was a mercy.

That first day on the road we saw many other muleteers with cargoed beasts, and Don Carmelo was happy, for he knew many of them. He sang along the way. I grew weary by midday, walking behind and watching to see that the loads did not slip on the animals. When this happened, they simply stopped and nothing could induce them to go forward. Don Carmelo knew this, and always made haste to adjust and tighten and balance the loads, though usually he would kick the mules viciously once they were loaded again.

By nightfall we had come to a village where there were many painted gypsy wagons, and here we joined the little caravan and unloaded and pegged out our mules to browse. I was expected to help at this. I was half falling with fatigue, and I wanted a rest and a good warm meal. But Don Carmelo disappeared at once and left me with the beasts. By moonrise I was wild with hunger. He did not return and I did not know what to do. Savory smells were drifting from the gypsy campfires; I watched until the fires were doused and the dancing began. All the gypsies gathered around a bare place in the grass, and there they started stamping and clapping their hands in rhythm.

There were men and women, exotically dressed, the women in skirts with many flounces and with ruffled sleeves, their hair tied with scarves and ribbons in brilliant colors. The men, too, wore silk blouses, though their tight trousers were of dark wool or of leather. One man sat on a chair, idly fingering the strings of a guitar. Suddenly he struck a chord, and as he did so I saw Don Carmelo leap into the circle, take a position, and start snapping his fingers. Soon a proud and beautiful young woman, with a dress all swirling skirts, came and took a disdainful pose very close to him. She slowly raised her arms, making movements with her fingers. Then they danced together, never touching each other. It was like watching the courtship of two beautiful birds or wild forest creatures. All the others were watching in silence, though occasionally someone snapped his fingers or clapped, or gave a hoarse cry in their own language.

It was a lovely sight there under the moon, the dancers occasionally outlined by a glow of firelight, as a fire threw up a flame or two before it died. But I was hungry and impatient.

When two other gypsies began to dance, I found Don Carmelo and begged him for something to eat. He gave me a great clout on the side of the head that made my ears ring.

"I'll give you a beating! That's the best way to put an empty stomach to sleep," he hissed at me, catching up a piece of wood from one of the cooking fires and starting for me.

"Let the little black go," advised a pretty gypsy girl, idly. "Save your strength for dancing."

Don Carmelo dropped his club.

"Learn to steal your food, like a Romany rye," he told me, "and I will teach you many useful tricks. But if you want to go hungry, sit and wait for your meal! It will not walk to you, I promise you that!"

I could not believe my ears, but it seemed that steal is precisely what he thought I should do. I stumbled back to where the mules were resting and made myself a little bed under a tree. Despite the growls of my protesting insides, I slept, but the next day I saw that I would have to take Don Carmelo's advice or die on the journey. He gave me nothing but an occasional crust or a bone from his own meal in all the days we traveled.

What could I do? I was a city child; I had been protected and, I now realized, loved. I had never known hunger or cold or neglect like this. Don Carmelo lived only for each sundown when he could find a gypsy encampment, or some gypsy café in town, and then he gave himself up to his leaping and dancing. How he managed, walking the roads all day and dancing until midnight, I do not know. He must have been made of steel. As for me, I stole fruit or cabbages, and once I found a loaf which had fallen from someone's pack, and I ate it ravenously, dry. But I could not slip into a field and milk a cow or a ewe; I did not know how. I could not catch a pigeon or a chicken and wring its neck, or set a snare for a rabbit, as Don Carmelo did.

But necessity, they say, is the best teacher. I soon learned to throw myself down and sleep with the beasts as soon as they were unloaded—in country, courtyard, or wherever we stopped—and then early, with the morning star, I rose, and I would go to sit, all doubled up, on the stairs of the nearest church, my hand held out for alms. I turned to begging, as Friar Isidro had done. With spirits elevated and hearts warmed by the service, many of the faithful dropped a *maravedi* into my palm, and sometimes I would collect enough at the church door to buy food for myself for all day. On bad days I simply went round and knocked on doors and pleaded for something to eat. I must have touched many hearts with pity, for I was by then in rags, thin, and frequently bleeding from some blow that Don Carmelo had dealt me.

By the time Don Carmelo had loaded his beasts (he was careful about this) and fed them and cooked his breakfast (often roasting a bird on a spit, or heating a sausage on a stick until it dripped fragrant fat sputtering into the fire) I would be back, having begged and bought my loaf hot from the bakeshop, or perhaps even a couple of eggs, which I cracked and drank raw.

Don Carmelo began to eye me with interest as I developed my own system for survival, and when it appeared to him that I was eating reasonably well, he demanded that I bring him a piece of bread every morning.

By now we had passed the dry dusty plains of La Mancha and were rising into the mountains. Nights began to be very cold. My shoes were worn through, and I had tied up my feet in rags, as many beggars did. I was often hungry again, as occasionally we had not found a village by nightfall and were forced to make camp in the country. Don Carmelo was as skillful as all his kind at this. He always found a sheltered place near water, protected by the brow of a hill or by tall trees. But when he had none of his own wild people near to divert him with their music, he amused himself by beating me.

I endured this until we came to a good-sized town, and there I decided to hide from him to make my way somehow to Madrid alone.

But my chance did not come easily. Gypsies can read one's thoughts, and Don Carmelo, I am sure, had no trouble reading mine. He was up as early as I, and before I had whined three *maravedis* into my palm he was upon me, had seized the collar of my now-ragged shirt, almost pulling it off in his hand, and hurried me along the street to the bakeshop. When I had bought my bread he took it from me and then went off swaggering down the street, whistling between huge mouthfuls. There was nothing for me to do but slink back to the church steps and try again, after the next Mass. But before I had gone more than a few steps, a huge hairy hand fell on my shoulder. I cringed, fearing that Don Carmelo had returned. But it was Don Dimas, the town baker.

"Do you belong to that gypsy?" he asked me, in a harsh whisper.

Now I was a slave, but also a snob.

"Since when can a gypsy own a black slave?" I asked scornfully. "Certainly not. Through adverse circumstances," I said, using words as long and as impressive as I could command, "I am in his caravan. He is taking goods to my master in Madrid. How far are we from Madrid?" I asked anxiously.

The baker, a great stupid-appearing man, wearing the dirty, white-dust-covered apron and cap of his trade, scratched his head.

"I don't really know," he muttered. "It's far away, I think. Nobody around here has ever been there."

"Why did you stop me just now?" I then asked.

"My boy is sick and I need a young fellow to shovel flour and help tend the oven."

"Let me, let me!" I begged, forgetting all about my fine airs, which, truth to tell, did not match my dirty rags and half-starved look. "Let me! Only don't tell Don Carmelo where I am. I would rather go to find my true master in my own time, and without that gypsy's kicks and blows all the way."

A little glimmer of greed began to shine in the baker's small eyes. But I was ready for it; I had seen that look before.

"For two loaves a day and a place to sleep," he offered.

"No. I must eat meat or cheese when you do, and have my two loaves, and also a good warm coat when I leave."

"How long will you stay?"

"Until your boy is better. Or . . . no." (It occurred to me that the boy might die, and I might be impressed into service for many months.) "No, I will work for you for forty days."

"Well . . ."

"On your word of honor that you will feed and pay me as I say," I demanded, "or I will run back to the gypsy right now."

"My word of honor, then."

I could see that he was flattered to be asked to give it.

"Before a witness," I insisted. God knows where I had got my ideas of legal protection, but the baker was stupid enough to be impressed, and he made quite a ceremony of stopping a crony of his in the street, a bleary-eyed stumbling fellow on his way to the wineshop, and demanding that he witness an oath.

And so I became the slave, temporarily, and of my own free will, of Don Dimas.

The gypsy did not do me the compliment of looking for me. And I soon found that my job was a hard one. The flour got into my eyes and my nostrils and made me cough, and the great iron pans we loaded and slid into the oven were terribly heavy. But I did get soup with an occasional piece of sausage, and during the day the ovens were comforting in their heat. I slept in a shed at the back, and I was glad it was not full winter or I should have frozen to death. The shed was made of slats held together with rawhide, and the wind that rose just before dawn whistled through the open spaces. But by then I was up and we were firing the ovens. I was mightily plagued with rats at night, though, and slept restlessly, turning on my little heap of straw, and fearing that the creatures might attack me. I was too naive; those rats were fat and sleek from feeding in the baker's own granary; their squeaking was just their talk as they went about their affairs at night. Though sometimes there were frightful shrieks and howls, and sounds as if devils were fighting. After the first evenings when this happened, startling me from slumber, I slept through, for these were the regular battles between the rats and the baker's cats. There were many of these, black, white, spotted and striped, and the baker never gave them anything to eat, his theory being the same as Don Carmelo's. The cats, made to fend for themselves, lived off the rats and kept the rodents from ruining the baker altogether.

The baker had a pale and sickly wife, as well as the ailing child, and though they took no special care of me and seldom spoke to me, I felt sorry for them and for the harassed baker himself. But I did not waver in my plan of getting to Madrid, and when my time was up I went to ask for my coat and to say good-by.

I was given a coat; the baker's wife had made it for me, using some old scraps of cloth in her chest. It was a curious garment, made entirely of patches, some large, some small, but it was all wool and I was glad to have it. I begged an old sack for my loaves (I had saved seven against my journey, so as to be sure of something to eat on the way) and took my leave.

The road to Madrid wound away toward the north and I believed that I would surely reach some town before nightfall, but I did not. I had to lie that night in the open, cold and scared. But I munched on one of my loaves, and somehow I got through. By noon of the next day I came to a village, and there I learned that Madrid was still five days' traveling ahead.

There were a few people on the highways, and whenever I could I stayed close behind some merchant or well-to-do gentleman. On the third day I followed a young man who rode one horse and led another, carrying his baggage behind on a mule. At the end of the day I approached him and asked to watch over his animals at night, and run along by his side during the day.

He was blond and handsome, and he turned on his horse, sitting sideways, and looked at me with curiosity.

"How does it happen that such a ragged little blackamoor speaks such good Spanish?" he asked me.

"I am the slave of a gentleman," I told him proudly, "and I was brought up in an aristocratic house. That's where I learned my Spanish."

"With a Sevillian accent," he mused. "Why are you marching north, and alone? Are you a runaway?"

"No." I would say no more, out of caution.

He was sunk in thought, but then he said, "Very well. You may travel with me."

We slept under the stars that night, and continued next day. His horses seemed to eat the miles, though the young gentleman did not hurry them but kept them at a steady walk. When he made a nooning, he gave me cheese and wine, and I solemnly offered to share my loaf. That night he stopped at an inn, and I was allowed to sleep in the stables. So we continued, and my hopes rose. I began to dream of Madrid, of clean clothes, and a pleasant house once more, even though I would be a slave. Freedom, I had learned on the highways, is hard defended, and all along the way the weak fall victims to the strong.

On the fourth night, we came to an inn. After I had unburdened the mule and unsaddled the horses and rubbed them down, and watered and fed them in the patio, the young gentleman called me to his side.

"You have been a good boy," he said to me kindly, "and I have been glad of your company. But now we must part, for I cannot ride into Madrid with a slave. Nobody would believe you were not mine, and you have no papers to prove where you belong. You would be taken from me and sold, for I have many debts and many creditors. I would spare you that. Here is a *real* for you; put it in your belt or hide it. And good luck to you."

I never learned his name, and I never saw him again. I wish that I had. But before the next day's dawn had broken I had forgotten him and everyone else, and could think of nothing but my pain.

I lay in the stable near his horse, but in the darkness, while I was deeply asleep, a hand fell on me, and I was jerked to my feet. In the fitful light of a lantern, a little distance away, I saw the teeth of Don Carmelo, bared in his cruel smile, and I heard his hissing as he beat me.

"Run away . . . would you . . . and let me go to Madrid without you, little black toad! Don Diego refused to pay me one cent until I had brought you! All my work and the weary miles for nothing . . . and then the bother of searching for you . . . spider's child! Now you will come with me to Madrid and tied to my saddle horn!" He had a leather whip and he scourged me with it unmercifully, until I fell to the ground unconscious. I do not remember much of what happened after. Vaguely I recall the road, as half-dazed I stumbled along, tied to his saddle. My clothes stuck to the dried blood on my back and arms; my face burned where the whip had caught me and left bloody weals. I remember thirst and fever and the throbbing pains. Of Madrid I remember nothing at all. Only one more scene remains in my memory.

I wakened, and it was dark. I must have been hiding behind household gear and bales and boxes in a patio. Everything hurt me and I could hardly think. I could force my mind to nothing except the determination to remain quiet and hidden.

Then I heard steps and the flashing of a hand lantern darting here and there among the boxes. I was in terror of being found and beaten again. But a voice called, "Juanico! Come out. Please. The gypsy who hurt you has been sent away."

I could not believe it, but the lantern found me out, and then shone full upon me where I crouched.

"Poor child, come inside. We must feed you and bathe those wounds."

I was lifted and led into a warm kitchen. First I was given a bowl of chopped meat and onions; nothing ever tasted so good to me. Gratefully I ate it, thinking of nothing further away than my spoon. I was still sobbing and hiccuping with fear. Gradually I became conscious of a quiet presence near me. Looking up, I saw a very young man, with a cloud of black hair, and deep-set eyes which looked at me gravely. He was short and slender and wore good dark clothes but no jewels of any kind. I supposed that he must be a secretary or a clerk in the household.

"Tell me," I stuttered, "is Master good? Is he kind? Will he beat me? Oh, what will happen to me here?"

"You will be healed and washed and given new clothes. You will never be beaten again."

"But Master, what will he do with me?"

"I am the Master, Juanico. I will take care of you. You will learn to help me. You will be useful here in my house, but your tasks will not be too hard."

It was a long speech, I learned later. Master never spoke much.

I still trembled and cried out when my bloody clothes were taken from me, opening the wounds of my beating and making me bleed anew. The home medicine of fresh vinegar and beef suet, which was applied to them, stung and I was in pain and misery all the night. But I was clean. I lay on fresh straw covered with white sheets in a warm alcove, off the kitchen. And I was safe.

Four

In which I learn my duties

WHAT do I remember of my youth? I remember Master and his studio.

Within a week I was quite well and had been given new clothes. They pleased me, for Master did not dress me up like a pet monkey in bright silks and turbans as Doña Emilia had done in her innocent fancy. He was an austere man himself, uninterested in furbelows except when he had to paint them. He bought me a good, serviceable jacket and knee trousers of country-woven wool, dyed dark brown. I felt a momentary quiver of distaste as I saw my brown hands and wrists emerging from the brown stuff; I thought I must look in this suit as if I were covered with a second skin. Master himself stood back and stared at me with his detached, impersonal regard.

"One gold earring came among my aunt's things," he said suddenly. "It would look well on you."

"Perhaps it is the other of a pair that were my mother's," I told him. "Mistress gave me one, but I lost it on the road. She told me she would keep the other for me."

No doubt the gypsy had stolen my earring as I lay unconscious. My *real* was gone, also.

Master brought the earring, and I took it with reverence and worked it through the hole in my ear. It was my mother's; I was glad to feel it bobbing against my cheek. Master looked pleased to see the sparkle of gold against all the brown.

I wore that hoop for many years, until I sold it one day in Italy. But that was much later. I will tell you about that in good time.

Our household was a simple one, but ample and comfortable. The Mistress, Doña Juana de Miranda, was a round, bustling little woman, very active and competent in managing everything. She had a cook and a housemaid, between whom she divided all the household chores. I wondered just how much she would require of me, but I had no qualms, and I was determined to be trustworthy and careful and to do whatever she wished. I gave thanks daily that I had found a good Master and that I would never again be in the power of creatures like Carmelo.

I ate in the kitchen with the cook, who soon pampered me with tidbits, and I had a small room to myself, off the kitchen. It had been made for the pot boy and stable help, but Master kept neither horse nor carriage. He walked when he had to go somewhere, and Mistress hired a carriage once a week to make her calls and go shopping.

However, I soon found that I was not to do anything but serve Master, and he did not even want me to help him dress or to lay out his clothes. I brushed them and rubbed oil into his belts and boots, but Mistress herself, like a good wife (and I suspect because she adored him, and loved to work over and touch his things), sewed and mended his linen and saw that it was fresh. Master had other plans for me.

He had allowed me to rest and heal in those first days in his home. As soon as I was well, he said, "Come," and he took me into his studio.

This was a large room on the second floor of the house. It was almost bare, with a great window to the north that let in a pure cold light. Several easels, strong and sturdy, stood about, a chair or two, and there was a long table with a palette on it, a vase full of brushes, rags, and bits of canvas and wood for frames. In winter the studio was bitter cold, and in summer it was hot as an oven. During the heat it was full of smells, as well, for with the windows flung wide open, there ascended to us from the street the odor of refuse, of horse dung, and of tanning leather, for there was a leather craftsman near by. The smells were awful, but Master never noticed anything . . . heat nor cold nor bad smells nor dust. All he thought about was light, and the only days when he was nervous were days of low fog or rain that changed the light he lived by.

One by one, he taught me my duties. First, I had to learn to grind the colors. There were many mortars for this work, and pestles in varying sizes. I soon learned that the lumps of earth and metallic compounds had to be softly and continuously worked until there remained a powder as fine as the ground rice ladies used on their cheeks and foreheads. It took hours, and sometimes when I was sure the stuff was as fine as satin, Master would pinch and move it between his sensitive fingers, and shake his head, and then I had to grind some more. Later the ground powder had to be incorporated into the oils, and well-mixed, and much later still, I arranged Master's palette for him, the little mounds of color each in its fixed place, and he had his preferences about how much of any one should be set out. And, of course, brushes were to be washed daily, in plenty of good Castile soap and water. Master's brushes all had to be clean and fresh every morning when he began to work.

Much later, I had to learn to stretch cotton canvas to the frames, and when I had learned the trick of it, I was set to doing the same with linen. This was, for me, the hardest task of all.

Master had all the tools for framing the canvas sharpened and put into good order and bought me plenty of wood to practice with. Each time I built a frame and stretched a canvas, holding the frame taut with wooden pins, and nailing the canvas on around the frame, he showed me the flaws in my work by his expression. For some time the trouble was with my carpentry. My corners didn't fit, or the side pieces were not precisely to measurement, or the pegs were too clumsy. Oh, it took care and thought, and I shed many tears. Doña Emilia had never asked more of me than to fan her or hand her a sweet or hold her parasol, until she taught me to write. But this work was a man's, and I grieved that I could not learn it.

One day when I had failed for the third time at trying to fit a frame on which he wanted to stretch a good linen canvas, Master put down his palette, left his model fretting on the model stand, and showed me just how. His fingers were slim and sensitive, with dark hairs on the second knuckle; his nails were almond-shaped. Many a woman would have been proud to have such delicate hands as his. He cut and fitted the pieces precisely, so easily, so quickly, that I lost heart. I had spoiled so many. I put my head in my hands and sobbed.

He lifted my head at once, smiled briefly, a mere flash of white teeth under the small dark mustache, and hurried back to his easel. I took the wood and the tool, held them just as he had and tried again, and this time it came right. I never failed again, and from then on I stretched all his canvases.

But this was but the beginning. Once properly stretched on the frame, the cloth had to be prepared to take the paint. We had many coatings we put on; Master taught me all the formulae from memory. In an access of enthusiasm, I told Master I could write and that I would note down all the preparations.

"No," he said. "These are professional secrets. Keep them in your head."

And so I had to train my memory for each sort of finish to spread on the canvas, according to what use Master would have for it.

He usually rose and had his breakfast by six, earlier in summer. His breakfast was always the same: a piece of grilled meat and a small trencher of bread. Occasionally he would take an orange into the studio, and there eat it thoughtfully as he planned his work for the day. He liked the early light when it was still fresh from the dew and without any dancing dust motes in it. He was always in the studio until the light went in the afternoon, but he was not always painting. He made drawings, many drawings, though he did not save them, but tossed them aside. (I was able to keep a few.) He drew so much, so easily, so perfectly, that when at last he stood before a frame of prepared canvas, he could sketch in the outlines of his subject in one moment of flashing charcoal, never having to correct more than a knife-edge of line.

And often he simply sat staring . . . now at a piece of draped velvet, now at a copper bowl, now at me.

When I felt a little more confidence in his presence, and did not fear disturbing him in one of his reveries, I asked him why he did this.

"I am working, Juanico," was his answer. "Working, by looking."

I did not understand and so I held my tongue, thinking that this was what he meant me to do with this cryptic answer. But a week or more later, he spoke to me as if I had put my question but a moment before, answering, "When I sit and look at something I am feeling its shape, so that I shall have it in my fingers when I start to draw the outline. I am analyzing the colors, too. For example, do you see that piece of brocade on the chair? What color is it?"

"Blue," I answered promptly.

"No, Juanico. There is a faint underlay of blue, but there is violet in that blue, the faintest touch of rose, and the highlights are red and bright green. Look again."

It was magical, for suddenly I could see them, the other colors, just as he said.

"The eye is complicated. It mixes the colors for you," explained Master. "The painter must unmix them and lay them on again shade by shade, and then the eye of the beholder takes over and mixes them again."

"I should like to paint!" I cried out in my joy at this revelation.

"Alas, I cannot teach you," said Master, and then he became silent again and returned to his easel.

I pondered this remark and lay awake at night thinking of it after dark, for I could not understand why he could not teach me. I decided that he had meant to say, "I will not teach you," or "I do not wish to teach you." I put this thought away deep in my memory because it made me so sad. I had begun to love him, you see, and to wish to offer him all my heart's loyalty. But these words were a little worm, gnawing away at my affection.

The thought kept coming into my mind as I ground colors, or moved a vase or a flower jug when he was painting, or stretched linen on a frame. Perhaps he was simply too busy? That could be. Or perhaps he hated teaching. That could be, also. Then one day I learned the reason, but not from him.

Our life was very tranquil. Mistress was a careful and thrifty woman who watched over all the expenses of the household and was always busy mending or sewing or working at her tapestries. She was merry and gay, too, and often sang as she went about the rooms. The children, two little girls, Francisca and Ignacia *(la niña)* were toddlers, and very endearing, with their big soft eyes and their baby prattle. Master often held them on his knee, silently studying them, feeling the curve of the tender baby cheeks with his fingers. I would have been happy to help care for the little ones, but I was seldom asked to do it. It was accepted in our house that I belonged to Master. This suited me well, and in all except that little nagging wish to paint, I was content, having every reason to look forward to a pleasant and comfortable life.

The rooms of the house were large, well-carpeted, and with shutters to hold out the strong sun of summer and the bleak wind of winter. The curtains and the chairs were of red velvet mostly, with here and there an occasional note of sober deep blue. There was a crucifix over each bed, even mine, and when it was very cold there were many brasiers in the rooms, giving off a delicate but pervasive heat from glowing coals. There were no paintings by Master about. The walls were covered with rugs or hangings; all Master's work was kept in the studio.

One day Mistress called me and asked me to help her tidy a great carved chest she had at the end of her bed, in which I supposed she might have stored blankets and other woolen things, against the winter. But when she lifted the lid I saw a rainbow of silks in many colors that had been rumpled and stuffed back just any way.

"Help me fold these, Juanico," she directed me. "Then we will arrange them, all the darker shades at the bottom, and brighter ones toward the top. Your Master will keep this chest in his studio and you are to see that the stuffs are always in order, and bring them to him whenever he wants a spot of color, or a background of some cloth to catch the light. You will be very busy helping him now, for he is going to take in some apprentices."

"I thought he did not like to have apprentices about," I faltered.

"The court has asked him to do so," she told me. "Your Master is very deeply obligated to certain men of the court and could not refuse. Besides, he has many church commissions now and cannot do them all. He will have to have help, for backgrounds and so on, and perhaps even to make copies of his works."

"I wish I could learn to paint also!" I blurted out, forgetting that I had promised myself not to mention the matter again.

"I wish you could," Mistress answered, "but there is a law in Spain which forbids slaves to practice any of the arts. The crafts, some manual skills, yes. But not art. However, do not grieve. Move back now, and do not let your tears fall on this taffeta; they will spot it. I know you love color, Juanico. You may help me choose the colors for my embroidery, and I will ask Master to give you sole charge of this chest."

I remembered that Mistress had been daughter of a great painter before she became wife of one, and so I took her word.

So that was why I would not be taught to paint, could never transfer my vision to canvas. I felt sad, but I did not feel, at that time, any resentment at being a slave. God knows I was happy with Master and Mistress. I felt useful and appreciated. Freedom? I had had a taste of it on the road, and it was cruel to a black boy. I swallowed my disappointment, and as I dragged the laden chest through the halls to the studio I felt a kind of comfort. Master had not denied me of his own free will, but because he was forced to do so, by the law.

That very day we began to make ready a room for the apprentices to live in. A carpenter was called to come and fill in walls where some old stables stood open on one side, in the back patio. He was a merry fellow, singing as he cut and fitted his lumber, and in a few days there were two snug little rooms, each with a wide wooden bench to sleep on and a good chest with a lock, in which the apprentices could keep their possessions. I would have liked a chest with a lock, too, but none was given me, and so I supposed that this, too, was something slaves could not have. I therefore put the matter out of my mind and devoted myself to the tasks at hand.

The apprentices were, of course, free white boys, but they were under special obligations to Master and bound to obey him, just as I was, and in truth I had more freedom than they, for I was part of the household. I had Master's confidence, and he revealed himself to me in many small intimate ways. The apprentices were kept on a footing of severe formality. We all called him Master, slave and white boys alike, for Master means Teacher, Authority, Chief.

One of our apprentices was only a few years older than I, about sixteen. He was round-faced, pink-cheeked and blue-eyed, with blond hair and he had the most innocent smile in the world. His name was Cristobal; his father was a carver of religious images. We all thought Cristobal a simple soul, at first. But he was a schemer and a trouble maker, and it was soon clear why his father had not taken him on as one of his own apprentices, to learn the family skill.

Cristobal was a liar and a thief. He used to take things and then try to pretend that I had stolen them. Master set a trap and caught him at this, and promised to send him home to his father for a good whipping the next time anything of the sort happened. Then Cristobal let me be, though sometimes he could not resist pinching me or tripping me.

Once when Cristobal stole a piece of Master's azure silk, I was in hopes he would get rid of the boy for good, but he merely sent him to bed without supper. Master never beat anyone. I think he kept Cristobal because the boy was remarkable at drawing. He could sketch swiftly, catching the movement of a bird on the wing or a cat leaping after a drifting feather with but a few telling lines, and he could suggest a likeness which seemed to me miraculous in one so young.

I heard Master and Mistress talking about the apprentices one evening after supper, as Master sat with his glass of ruby wine and a few raisins.

"Send him home," suggested Mistress. "He makes me nervous and I am afraid he will hurt one of the babies."

"No, for they would cry and point him out. He is a real sneak," said Master sadly.

"I don't like him."

"Nor do I. But he has a remarkable talent."

"What about the other one, Alvaro?"

"A good boy. Dutiful, well-mannered, correct. He will never be a painter, though. A good copyist, perhaps."

Alvaro was the son of a scrivener at court. He was little and thin and he stuttered. Also, he had a delicate stomach. I liked Alvaro, but I paid more attention to Cristobal. I had to, in order to protect myself, my clothes, and the things which Master had put into my charge.

When Master had a portrait commission (and at certain times

of the year he had many) I had to be near to arrange tables and chairs on the model's dais; I had to have good sketching paper ready, fixed firmly against a backing of light wood. I had to provide well-burned charcoal sketching sticks. To make them, I built a little fire and closed it in with bricks, all but a small vent, in the back patio, and then I toasted thin twigs and branches of olive until they were charred through.

Always I had to adjust the windows, so as to keep the light striking the same spot on a lady's gown or a gentleman's coat. It was very delicate work, and I had to be most attentive.

Master was curiously exacting about all of these matters, but when the sitting began, I alone knew how strange he was about his work. He always kept a drape that could be let down over his canvas, so that no one could see what he was doing; he never allowed sitters to see his paintings until they were finished. Many times, days would pass, and Master had done little more than stand and think, in front of a model, sometimes drawing a line or two.

And yet when he had decided upon every detail in his mind, when he had thought out the whole composition and had analyzed all the colors and lines, then he seized his brush and worked swiftly. He held the brush about four inches above where the hair began, and his palette—a large, smooth, kidney-shaped piece of wood—was always prepared with small mounds of colors in an unchanging order. Nearest his thumb were the cool, earth colors, gradually becoming warmer and more glowing until they ended in a larger mound of white. When Master was working intensely, he did not even glance at his palette, but put his brush unerringly into the colors he wanted, taking the amounts he needed and blending them in the middle to the shades he required. I have seen him thus mix up the same shade time and time again, without glancing, and taking them straight to the canvas; they were always perfect.

His strokes on the canvas, too, sometimes seemed slapdash, rough and unintelligible, if one stood as close to the canvas as he. But a little distance away, and those spots and dashes of light cream or ivory would resolve themselves into a delicate frill of lace, or the daintiest of highlights on satin. Time after time I verified this, and it always seemed magical to me. Master never commented on my astonishment, but often I saw a slight smile curl the quiet mouth beneath the dark silky mustache.

And he never chatted while he worked. It was the sitter who spoke, and Master merely put in a word now and again, should there come an expectant silence. Then he would murmur, "Ah?" or "Possibly," or "Just so."

But he studied people. Once he said to me, when the sitter had gone home, and Master was working on a background, "I like to watch people when they talk about themselves, Juanico. Then they reveal to you what they really are. Women, for instance, love themselves; they speak of themselves as if they were talking about a beloved relative who is to be pardoned any foolishness. Men, on the other hand, seem to admire themselves. They speak of themselves like judges who have already brought in a verdict of 'Not guilty.'"

I ventured, "Isn't it difficult to show people their true selves when you paint them, Master?"

"No. Nobody ever knows what he really looks like. Bring me some more of the ochre."

And he was silent again.

Once in a while he would paint me, to keep his hand in, or would ask me to model some difficult fabric.

After he had taught the apprentices to draw vases and fruits and cheeses and hams and all manner of objects, he began to let them sketch people. Then I was often told to pose for them. Then I had my revenge on Cristobal and I helped Alvaro, turning myself subtly so as to ruin Cristobal's drawing and holding myself very still when I noticed Alvaro's eyes on me. Master scolded me for this and watched me, but all the same I was sometimes mischievous. I was always sorry when Master criticized Alvaro's work and praised Cristobal's, and one day he answered the distress he saw that this caused me, by telling me his reason.

"Art must be true," he said. "It is the one thing in life that must rest on solid truth. Otherwise, it is worthless."

Then one day there was a knock at the door, and soon after, Mistress came running into the studio, pale with excitement. Behind her, pacing slowly, followed a messenger from the King. He handed a rolled parchment to Master, bowed, and turned. Mistress ran ahead of him to open the door for his departure. The apprentices and I stood silent and respectful as Master unrolled the parchment and read it. He rolled it up again, and took up his palette and brush once more. I remember that he was painting a bronze vase, and I had been at great pains to keep moving it so that the sunlight should continue to strike it at the same point every moment.

"Diego!" burst forth Mistress. "Tell me, please! Don't make me wait to know! What was in the King's message?"

"I am to paint his portrait," he answered at length, frowning.

"Oh, God be praised! How wonderful!"

"And I am to be given a studio in the palace."

Mistress collapsed onto a chair, which creaked ominously, and she had to fan herself. Little black curls escaped from her pompadour and fell down over her forehead. This meant she was to move in court circles. It meant a fortune, dignity, honors, position beyond anything she had dreamed of.

But Master was silent and pale as he continued to paint the vase. At last he murmured, under his breath, and only I heard, "I hope they haven't sent some courtier to select and prepare a studio for me. It must have light. Light. Nothing else matters. . . ."

Five

In which Rubens visits our court

IT was a confused and exciting time, but at last all of Master's easels and painting things and the chest of silks and his vases and chairs and draperies were moved to the studio in the palace and we began our work there.

Our house was in the heart of Madrid, not far from the Plaza Mayor, on Jeronimas Street. Every morning at first light, with hot breakfast in our stomachs, we cut through the Plaza and made our way to the palace. The guards soon learned to know us and to clash their swords together so that we could pass under them. Then we walked through the long silent corridors, which were always cold despite the fine tapestries and banners which lined the walls. We went up a broad stairway and down another arcade and so came to our studio, where there was always a guard in the King's livery. Master was in the service of the Crown.

And yet, for some weeks, we did not see his Royal Highness. We often saw his favorite, the big bluff Duke of Olivares, who stormed or stamped his way into the studio several times a day when he was in Madrid. He was swart and fat and exuded what looked like a greasy sweat; his black hair was seldom neatly combed and his big belly was always bursting the buttons off his jackets. The Duke was vulgar, I thought, and my instinct was to distrust him, for, despite his smiles and jovial laughter, he had mean little eyes. But I forgave him everything, as he seemed genuinely devoted to Master and constantly proclaimed that one day all Europe would echo to the name of Velázquez, greatest painter of them all.

I remember the day his Royal Highness appeared for his first sitting to Master. It was fall, and the sunshine which entered our studio was a pale golden with a touch of freshness. Two pages came first, blowing trumpets. There followed two other pages with standards, and then the King strode into the room. Most of us knelt on both knees; Master had dropped gracefully to one, and with his right hand he touched his jacket, above the heart.

The King was tall and very pale, with white-and-pink skin and hair like yellow embroidery silk. It was very light and shining clean, and it lifted and fell with each slow step he took. His shoulders were broad, but his legs were long and thin in their black silk stockings. His face was bony and rather sad. The smile he turned on Master was shy and seemed to ask for acceptance. Despite his fine clothes and all the people kneeling before him, despite the pages and the trumpets and the banners, I knew intuitively that he felt uncertain and that he hoped for friendship. Poor King, I thought, if you wish to make friends with Master. He is invariably kind, but he is taciturn and thinks of nothing but his painting. He will not talk to you.

But Master's quietness, his few gestures, and infrequent words perhaps were a comfort to the King, as he began coming often to the studio, for His Majesty must have had to put up with many endless hours of frivolous talk and of hollow praise. No doubt he had learned not to trust the golden words of courtiers.

Master's first portrait of the King was a plain study of his head only. He had the great craggy-featured face turned slightly, but the wary, pale blue eyes looked straight toward the painter. The mouth above the heavy, underslung jaw, was set, the lips unsmiling. Even that first portrait showed Master's perceptions; it was the face of a distrustful, but tender and hopeful, man.

Those hours of the King's sitting were very strange. The studio was always emptied for him; only I had to be on hand to give the Master a fresh charcoal or a new pot of freshly mixed colors. The King very early gave orders that we were excused from obeisances; we had only to make our first bows when he came in. Master used to stand motionless, looking and studying. Sometimes he would work intensely. There was absolute silence. I hovered about as inconspicuously as possible, most careful not to intrude my presence by any sound. Once when I felt a sneeze coming on I nearly died trying to suppress it, and when it overpowered me, explosive beyond all reason, shattering the calm, I felt as if I had committed a crime. Master said nothing and did not even glance at me. As for the King, he broke pose and, through some mysterious association, I suppose, took a lacy handkerchief from inside his sleeve and blew the Royal nose.

Occasionally Master would arrange his morning so as to be free for a little while shortly before noon. Then he would ask me to accompany him to one of the upper floors of the palace, from a window of which he could look out into the far distance.

"Space is medicine for eyes that have always to look at things too closely," he told me. "Those far mountains rest me. And I like to study the light."

When he was ready to descend, he would bring his eyes round and rest them thoughtfully upon me, and I could always

watch them changing focus. His eyes were very dark and deep-
set, so that it was hard to tell what he was thinking. Besides,
he disciplined and controlled his face, making it impassive.
Spaniards are said to be excitable, impetuous people, but that
is a lie. Master was as coolly dispassionate as a portrait himself,
with a face that did not change expression.

So we passed the day, except for Master's dinner hour with
his family. I now ate with Cook, for the apprentices were looked
after at the palace. Sometimes Master was summoned to some
state dinner or court function by the King; of course he could
never refuse these invitations. He never betrayed his impatience, but I could feel the reluctance in his fingers as he gave
me his brushes to wash or surrendered his palette. Often he
would sigh, but he always obeyed with his customary grave
courtesy. The only person who shook him and occasionally
caused him to bite his lip, as if biting back some irritated comment, was the rough-and-ready Duke of Olivares, who broke
into quiet conversations and disturbed silent sittings with all
the grace of a big plowhorse that has been made a pet, and is
always certain that people will be happy to see him, no matter
how many rosebushes he tramples.

Winters in the studio were harsh. Master would allow no heat
in there at all, and I often wondered how he continued to paint,
with his hands so cold. The apprentices had knitted gloves with
the fingers cut off at the tips. At home, Mistress always wore her
muff hung by a ribbon around her neck, and when she was not
busy she thrust her hands into it. As for me, I asked Cook for a
basin of hot water, and there I would soften and warm my
hands until I could move them again, after a long frozen day in
the studio.

But we were warm at night. Mistress gave us all warm woolen
covers, and at the evening meal she and Master sat with their
feet under a long felt tablecloth that came to the floor, and inside she set a brasier of glowing coals, to keep their legs warm.
The little girls were kept in bed a lot, and allowed to run about
only when there was strong sunshine.

Then softly, gradually, the cold receded from the air, the wind
blew less icily from the snow-topped mountains, the stones of
the palace released their frozen breaths, and spring came, with
rain and puddles, splashing and mud. Ah, but I loved it. Suddenly the world of sound was ours again all day as people
shouted in the streets, merchants called their wares, and horses
and carriages clattered by. And Master unwound the scarves he

had been wearing around his neck all winter and shed, one by one, the heavy garments that had given him a false appearance of corpulence.

With summer, the blazing heat came glaring down at us from a cloudless sky and it was fashionable to gasp and fan oneself and pretend to be overcome. But not in our house! We were Sevillanos, and loved the coppery summer sun. Master worked then in a lawn shirt, with free arms, and sleeves rolled above the elbow, making great round movements with his brush. He always painted prodigiously in summer.

So the years began marching past and I grew older. This I knew, for it began to be necessary for me to shave. Master gave me a fine razor with a blade of Toledo steel, like the one he used. And my voice deepened and grew resonant. Master loved to hear me singing as I went about my work.

I remember now a day in 1628. His Majesty arrived, preceded by pages and trumpeters, dressed in a costume of sea blue velvet, with a wide lace collar. He was not often so formal. Master sensed some announcement of great ceremony, and he put down his brush and palette and dropped onto one knee, to await it.

The King raised him, one delicate white hand on Master's black velvet shoulder.

"The painter Rubens, protected by the Regent of the Netherlands, is coming here to visit our court," he said, in his soft, stuttering voice, with its slight lisp. "He will bring a great retinue of servants and slaves, and I am assigning them all apartments in the palace. Rubens is, they advise, the greatest painter in Europe. I would like you, Don Diego, to be his guide and mentor during the days he is with us here in Madrid."

"It will be my honor," answered Master.

The King went on, "I shall give a reception and a banquet on the first evening of Rubens' arrival, to be followed by a court ball. I trust that Mistress Velázquez will be well enough to attend."

The King turned and was about to leave; the trumpeters put their golden instruments to their lips, but the King came back and once more laid his jeweled hand on Master's shoulder.

"I don't see how he could be a better painter than you, Diego. I don't believe he is. But we will accord him what he expects."

"I shall be glad to learn from him," said Master, simply.

I supposed that Master was merely being polite, for courtesy was natural to him, but once more I learned something about the man to whom I belonged. He accorded his art the highest respect, that of never taking it for granted. Always, as long as he lived, he tried to learn more, in order to serve it better.

The very next day, after the first great state banquet and reception, Rubens came to visit Master's studio. He was a great, florid, handsome man, broad in the shoulders and in the girth, with curly reddish-gold hair and a golden beard and mustache. After the first bows and compliments, they had me running my legs off bringing new brushes and freshly stretched canvases and paint rags, so that Rubens could demonstrate how he painted hair, how he dealt with fabrics, and how he built up those glowing flesh tones for which he was so famous.

They spoke easily together. Rubens was fluent, though he had a thick tongue for our language.

"Can you get in a nude model, a woman?" asked Rubens easily. "I could then give you a real illustration of my methods."

Master drew back. Our court was puritanical, and Master never painted from the nude.

"That would not be possible," he explained. "His Majesty is very delicate about such things. We might visit the studio of an image-maker I know of, who sometimes uses lightly draped male models, though our sinewy, sunburned country folk who model are not likely to show the porcelain and rose flesh tones your own canvases display," he added deprecatingly.

"My patrons have often spoken to me about the gifts of these religious image-makers in Spain," commented Rubens, eagerly. "I would like to watch one of them working."

It was the Duke of Olivares who arranged for them to go the next day to the studio of Gil Medina, a man who had many apprentices working in wood and in stone. I went along, carrying Master's sketchbook.

Because of the religious character of his work, a convent had set aside one of its great inner patios for the use of Master Medina. It was a splendid place to work, especially as some of the images were very tall and would have made excessive demands on the ceiling of even very large rooms.

The Duke of Olivares swaggered forward with his rolling gait and tossed his wide-brimmed plumed dark green hat back on his head, so that the feathers hung down on his collar. A gnarled and ferret-faced little man, not so tall as I, came forward and bowed low to him.

Presenting him, the Duke said, "This is our sculptor, a devoted Christian, and the best wood-carver in Europe. Don Gil, this is the great Peter Paul Rubens, painter to the Regent of the

Netherlands. And our own court painter, Don Diego Rodríguez de Silva y Velázquez."

The image-maker rubbed his hands together and murmured, "How can I serve your worships?"

Rubens answered. "I would like to see your work. But do not disturb yourself. I will wander around."

"You are in your own home," answered Gil Medina, in the Spanish fashion.

I remained a little distance away, observing the apprentices as Master and Rubens strolled. Most of them were small boys, not yet six. They were learning to carve on marked lines, using soft wood. The older ones, more skillful, were sitting at tables and working on large designs. There were a few tables covered with careful drawings, to scale. Standing about against the walls were all sorts of images, from Our Lady and the saints, in flowing robes, angels ready to launch out into the air on their great feathered wings, to crucifixes. The latter, and a few images of St. Sebastian and of another saint I could not identify, were the only figures shown unclothed except for modesty drapes. I saw Rubens stop and examine these with detailed care, running his fingers over the carving, standing back to enjoy the perfect proportions. I could not hear all his words, but when the Duke of Olivares answered him I made out everything; that booming voice would have carried a full league.

"Why, I often send Master Medina a criminal sentenced to death or to the galleys, so that he may work directly from life. Our country people are usually too proud to pose in this way. But if a man has been sent to the galleys, he is glad to have a few years knocked off his sentence, and I arrange that if he is willing to oblige our image-maker by being crucified for a few hours, or stretched on the rack. Master Medina gets those wonderfully agonized expressions from the faces of real men, I assure you! Of course we never really nail anybody to the cross, but even suspended, with strong cloth, the torture is excruciating!"

I, Juan de Pareja, heard those words with my own ears, and my heart sank. But Rubens answered calmly.

"So the thieves were crucified," he said. "Not with nails, but merely by suspension on the cross."

"Quite so," answered Medina.

Rubens went on. "I understand how you study live models for expressions of the Christ while He yet lived. But," and he pointed to a great carving of the crucified, larger than life size, hanging upon the cross in the limp and utter resignation of the dead, "how do you get your inspiration for this?"

The Duke laughed his great roaring laugh and, leaning closer, whispered something to Master and to Rubens, which I did not hear. Then he signaled to them and took them with him into another corridor, and through a door into another patio. I started to follow, for I was ordered to keep close to Master at all times—I always carried a bag with extra handkerchiefs for him, and money, since a gentleman seldom carries coins about, and his sketching materials—but Master Medina held me back. The door closed behind Master and Rubens.

"Stay here. They will return," said Master Medina to me, and then he went about his work finishing the carving on an angel face. I sidled away, but before Master returned, one of the apprentices came up to me and whispered, "They brought in a dying man, and Master hung him up on the cross and he died there. We all sketched. The Duke saw to it."

I felt an overpowering fear.

The little apprentice laughed and looked at me slyly.

"He would have died anyhow; he was condemned to the torture and to death. So we got the good of him."

Now they were returning from that inner court. Master's face showed no expression. And I could not ask about what I had been told. I wondered if I would ever know the whole truth of it. Perhaps the apprentice had lied, in order to enjoy my shock of horror. Young men often teased me in this way. I was a slave and had no defense against them. But I will be fair. I would not have fought them even if I had been free. I would have run from them . . . run far. Cruelty did always fill me with loathing.

We returned to the palace and Master dismissed me and told me I might go home and rest. I lay on my cot and tried to sleep, but I kept seeing, in a procession of visions, the faces of Gil Medina, weasle-eyed and avid, the suffering image of the Crucified, and the greedy, cruel young faces of the apprentices.

That night there was to be another banquet in the palace and I was to go in attendance on Master, so as soon as the sun dropped to the horizon I got up and washed myself and made myself presentable. Master was just emerging from his bedroom, dressed, as always, in black. This night his suit was of heavy brocade, and it was closed with glistening buttons of carved jet. A great collar of linen, so fine you could see your hand through it, lay on his shoulders. His soft dark hair was combed back from his brow and fell in waves to his neck. He wore no jewel of any kind.

"Good, Juanico. Come with me; we will go and see what the apprentices have been doing before we come back for Mistress. She does not feel well, but she insists upon attending the banquet. You must take a flask of strong perfume for her to breathe, and a fan."

When we stood before the work of the apprentices, Master studied what they had done. Then he took a brush and painted an annihilating red stroke through Cristobal's picture and stood silent (which was praise) before Alvaro's. They had been set to do a still life—a piece of moldy cheese, wine in a glass, and a hard crust of bread. Cristobal's painting was beautiful; the wine glowed ruby through the crystal glass, the cheese looked golden and creamy, and the bread was in shadow. Alvaro's showed the cheese dry and covered with green mold, as indeed it was, and further, he had painted a great ugly roach on it.

"Unimaginative Alvaro," commented Master, smiling. "There was a roach?"

"Yes, Master."

Oh, how foolish, I thought. He should have frightened it off, not painted it.

Cristobal was sulky.

"I would like to ask, most respectfully," he said, in a disrespectful tone, "why my painting was destroyed?"

"To teach you not to beautify. It is a great temptation."

Cristobal struggled not to say more, but he could not help himself. He looked at Master with rebellion in his bright eyes.

"I thought Art should be Beauty," he muttered.

"No, Cristobal. Art should be Truth; and Truth unadorned, unsentimentalized, is Beauty. You must learn this, Cristobal."

The boy was hurt and angry. Evidently he had loved his picture and expected praise. Alvaro, on the other hand, sat stunned behind his easel.

"Alvaro was honest, and his picture is full of truth. Say to yourselves, 'I would rather paint exactly what I see, even if it is ugly, perfectly, than indifferently paint something superficially lovely,' Say to yourselves, 'Art is Truth, and to serve Art, I will never deceive.'"

I don't know whether those boys remembered, but I have never forgotten.

Six

In which I fall in love

I HAVE been telling you about many people, but little about myself. Now, on this evening of the banquet, I shall direct your attention back to me, for something happened that I have carried in my heart all these years.

The banquet was a great formal dinner in the largest and most brilliant room of the palace. The lords and ladies who kept slaves had brought them, as was the custom, to stand behind their chairs and attend them at every moment . . . hand handkerchiefs, fan the ladies, or pick up a fallen hairpin. Some of the wealthy nobles were attended by relatives, but a great many people had a slave or two. I knew several young Negro slaves being trained to be valets to their owners, and the girls were often taught sewing and became skilled seamstresses, as was my mother; others were a kind of governess in the home, responsible for the children, and serving as nurse, when needed.

On this night, I saw, standing behind the chair of a lady in Rubens' train, a girl about my own age, delicately pale and dainty, but with the large dark eyes and tightly curling hair of my race. She had a stringed instrument in her hands, but they were free to play on the golden strings, for the lyre was held around her neck with broad silk ribbons.

When the meats had been eaten and taken away, and when the sweets and fruits were brought in, the girl's mistress signaled to her, and, steadying the instrument, the girl began to stroke chiming chords from it, while looking up, as if thinking and awaiting inspiration to begin. Then she began a strange, tremulous song in a voice as high and silvery as the notes she plucked from the strings.

I suppose the singer, an African in all her beauty, had lived among Arab peoples. She may even have had Arab blood. Her song was like their music, a wailing endless tune, each note shaped in her throbbing throat and then sent out to wind about in an elaborate tracery of wavering decorations. She sang with closed eyes, her face a mask of sorrow and longing. What was she thinking of—a lost home, dear ones she would never see again? I could not bear her song, beautiful as it was, for it was full of unanswered questions, and my heart was pierced with sadness.

When she finished, the company clapped for her with great

enthusiasm, and there was an undercurrent of excited comment. She merely waited with bowed head until all was silent again. Then she struck a few chords and immediately set up a rhythmic pulsing, and against this background she sent out a song in a thin, clear, high stream of sound, in a merry, mischievous voice. Now and again she would stop and beat a tattoo on the wood of her instrument with her fingers and the palm of her hand, and then she would look up at the company. When they demanded a third song, she sang a slow deep lament, intense and full of suffering.

I did not understand the language of her singing, and I had never heard music like hers before. And yet I understood it; it spoke to the blood that flowed in my veins, and told me of partings and farewells I seemed to know in my own flesh.

The next day I tried every way I knew to see the girl again. I made a thousand excuses to be near the corridors where Rubens' party were housed, but I had no luck. Only by chance did I learn that her name was Miri.

I thought of her constantly, and it was only with difficulty that I was able to carry out my duties. Master looked at me sharply several times, and more than once he had to repeat a request to me. Miri's face, her down-drooping head on the slender neck, her large dark eyes, her slender hands, the enchantment of her singing—these took up all my thoughts.

Soon after Mistress came in, to interrupt Master at his painting—for he was catching up on some work while awaiting word from Rubens about another visit he wished to make—to tell him that a note from Rubens had just been brought. While Master read it, Mistress looked at me; I was sighing as I ground some dark earth colors in a mortar.

"Juanico is in love, I think, Diego," she commented. "Poor child," she said, looking at me kindly. "Love is terrible."

I was struck speechless at what she said, but at once I knew it to be true. Yes, love was terrible, since it meant such suffering.

Master said, "Send the messenger away, please, my dear. I will send Juanico with an answer presently."

He went on painting for a half hour or so, while I was on fire to be off with his message in the hope of catching a glimpse of her. Then he calmly sat and wrote out a few words, signing them, as he did his infrequent letters, with a large "V."

I am sure that Master divined my passion and thought of sending me with the message so that I could be near the girl who had won my heart. I knew that he was kindly, but I did not realize then to what lengths he would go, in his quiet way, to give pleasure to others.

I took his note, but before I ran to Rubens with it I rushed away to wash my hands, dust my shoes and adjust my attire. How glad I was that Master dressed me like a man and not in the turbans and flowing robes of a fakir or a clown.

The guards passed me everywhere—they had only to note that "V" at the bottom of the message—and then at last only a large blond Dutch majordomo stood between me and Rubens. I demanded to be taken to the Master himself, at once. The majordomo bellowed something in Flemish, and at once there was an answering roar from inside. Rubens' voice.

"Let the boy in at once! I am expecting word from Master Velázquez!"

As I entered and before I saw the painter, a Dutch lady, trailing a light blue silken dress on the stones of the hall, rushed out of one of the rooms, carrying a basin. Another lady, in white, tried to comfort her, and I heard them murmuring together.

"What's the matter?" cried Rubens to them, and the one in white answered.

"It's the slave girl, Miri. She has had another attack, and her Mistress is distracted."

"Wait, I will add something to this note," Rubens told me. He sat and wrote hastily. "We need a doctor here. I hope your Master will see to it that a good one comes to us as soon as possible."

I ran all the way to our apartments in a turmoil of confusion, and arrived puffing and breathless.

"Go get Dr. Méndez and take him to Rubens," Master instructed me. "You know where he is."

Again I pounded forth. I had often fetched Dr. Méndez, for Ignacia was subject to fits of coughing that frightened Mistress half to death when they came upon *la niña.*

Dr. Méndez was a pale thin man, whose eyes were always circled with dark shadows. He looked as if he never got enough sleep, and perhaps he didn't. He was of a New Christian family, I knew, and was said to have all the lore of the great Jewish and Arabic physicians. The King was devoted to him also, and often consulted him.

I found Dr. Méndez in his laboratory, boiling something in a flask over a hot blue flame. His table was full of mortars and stewing pots and bottles of drugs. He made all his own medicines and unguents and would allow no one to help him for fear they might make a mistake. I had to wait until what he was doing had reached just the right point. Then Dr. Méndez put it away, put on his spectacles, and turned to me. I gave him the message. Then he hurried indeed, packing a little case in a moment and starting out of his door on the run.

When we came to the Rubens' apartments, I followed the doctor right into the sick room; in all the confusion, no one thought to stop me.

There was my beautiful Miri lying half-supported on a chair. Her head hung to one side, there was foam on her lips, and her eyes had rolled upward until only the whites showed. Her arms trailed down at her sides, and her hands shook and trembled on her wrists like blossoms on a delicate stem.

The doctor made a gesture which caused the fluttering ladies to stand back, and then he unstoppered a bottle and began to wave it under Miri's little nose. In a moment or so she moved her head, and then she gagged and coughed. He continued to follow her nose with the opened bottle until she straightened up and her eyes began to focus normally. She stared around her in a frightened way, and then great tears welled up in them and spilled over.

"Ay, Mistress," she cried, "did it happen again?"

The lady in blue came to her and took Miri's hand and pressed it kindly.

"It is only that you frighten me so, Miri!"

They spoke in the curious Spanish of the Flemish court, but I could understand them.

"I am so ashamed," sobbed Miri, dropping her face into her hands and trying to make herself very small in the big chair.

Dr. Méndez patted Miri's shoulder comfortingly, and packed away his vial.

"I could not have done much, anyway. It is the falling sickness, is it not?"

"Yes. She gives a terrible cry and falls, and then she writhes and her eyes go up and she foams. She seems to suffer so. . . . "

"There is no way to help her that we know," said Dr. Méndez sadly. "Try to make sure, when she gives her cry of warning, that she does not fall on something hard, or into a fire. And comfort yourself, madame. I do not think she really suffers except afterward, when she grieves that she has bothered and frightened you."

"I am so afraid," wailed Miri, "for I am a trouble and a disturbance for Mistress, and some day she will get tired of me . . . and sell me. . . . "

"Don't say such things, Miri," soothed her mistress. "There, there."

But Miri, my love, my beautiful one, wept on inconsolably.

I had been happy and grateful indeed that I had so kind a Master as Don Diego; I had not really been sad to be a slave, except for not being able to paint. Every life has some drawbacks. But I noticed that Miri's mistress had not promised not to sell her, and perhaps. . . . Like poor Miri, my heart constricted with fear. It was pierced with the thorn that lies close to the heart of every slave: will I be sold some day?

Even with my heart broken at parting, at knowing that I would never see Miri again (for they left the court soon after, to make their way to Italy, Rubens and all his train), that other fear that she had taught me persisted. Any distant singing, or silvery twanging on a psalter, brought that desolate cry into my mind: "Mistress will tire of me . . . and sell me. . . ."

Children, they tell me, often wake up crying, for they have dreamed that their mother or father is dead.

Often I woke up weeping and terrified now. . . . I had dreamed that I was sold.

Seven

In which I visit Italy

THE months went by, and at first I thought every day of Miri. But Time is a great traitor who teaches us to accept loss. I was young, and young hearts cannot always be sad.

We now had an apartment in the palace near the studio, where Master could rest, and where Mistress could come and sit with her sewing, and where the little girls could play and roll a ball about on the floor. The little daughters of Master were growing and becoming more lively and amusing every day. It was my hard task to keep them out of the studio, for they loved to follow their father there, pattering after him on their small feet.

In warm months Master did not always close the studio door, and there was no way to keep them out. I was always taking their warm little hands to lead them back to their mother, who often felt ill and listless and could not run after them all day.

The King was frequently in the studio, sitting for his portrait, and several times he was painted with a favorite hound at his feet. The hounds grew fond of me at the sittings, and I got the idea of getting a pet animal for Master's little girls to play with. Not a big dog. Perhaps a little one. Or maybe even a kitten.

One day I asked for permission to go and make my devotions at a church outside the palace, and Mistress gave me several errands to do. I was to go to the button merchant in the great market near the Puerta del Sol and choose six blue buttons for a frock she was sewing for one of the children, and I was also to find an herbalist and buy a small measure of dried leaves of the pink rose of Castile. Alvaro had wakened with his eyes swollen shut and inflamed, and could find no rest, so Mistress would make a tea of Castilian rose for him; it was wonderful for soothing and curing the eyes, and Master often bathed his eyes in the cooled tea from roses, to keep his sight keen.

I set out joyously, for church gave me great serenity and strength of spirit. I smelled the burning wax of the candles and the spicy fragrance of incense, and felt like a person who comes home where love awaits him. I joined my hands and said prayers for all my beloved dead, and also of course for Master and Mistress and the King. Lately I added a prayer for Miri, too. As I knelt, it seemed as if an angel folded me within his wings, shutting out all that was ugly or hurtful in the world.

It did not take me long to do the errands Mistress had requested, and afterward I set about finding a pet for Paquita, as Francisca was called.

The palace cooks had many cats to do daily battle with the rats, but they were strong fierce creatures, unused to petting. I had seen small fluffy kittens, so soft and tender inside their thick silky coats that when you lifted them, you could feel no more weight than a sparrow. These kittens were sold as pets; Arab traders brought them from somewhere in Asia Minor. They were most endearing little creatures, with round green or golden eyes and short pink noses. There was a lacemaker who had a shop near the Puerta del Sol, and I knew that she had a pair of these cats and often sold the kittens.

This woman was called Doña Trini. She had taken a fancy to me because she had seen me in the markets sometimes, and she claimed I was good luck for her; on the days she touched my coat, she said, she had wonderful business and many sales. She used to cry out to me, "Hola, Negrito! Come and cross my palm with your fingers, to bring me good fortune today!"

Now I was going to ask for my reward.

When I came to the door of her shop and looked in, she was busy selling a lace collar to a fine lady, but she interrupted herself to give me a flashing smile and to make a sign that I was to wait. I held my breath and concentrated my thoughts on her and wished her well, and my power was felt, because the lady bought three collars and counted out many golden doubloons into Doña Trini's hand. I stepped back, well out of the way as the lady left the shop; sometimes white people did not want me to step on their shadows, for fear of bad luck, and I was always careful not to frighten them.

"Negrito!" came a call from within. "Again you have brought me good luck! Come, and I will give you a date cake."

Doña Trini's wrinkled little face was very happy; she could live many weeks on her doubloons, and her small light eyes were snapping with good humor.

"Doña Trini," I said, "I thank you, but I want to ask you for something else. Not a date cake."

She was suddenly suspicious, thinking I intended to ask her for money.

"What thing, Negrito? I am a poor woman, and must pay out most of the money I was just now given for my three collars. But I will give you what I can because you are a talisman for me."

"I want a little white kitten."

She clapped her hands in pleasure and jumped up and down,

her wide brown and black skirts bouncing like a child's.

"You shall have one! A beauty! I sold the others of the litter, but this little one, the smallest, is the prettiest of all!" She ran into the back of her shop, where she worked at her lace and had her little bedroom and kitchen, and scooped up a bit of white fluff. I heard the mother cat's gentle protesting "Miaw?" as she did so.

"Look now, what a darling! No one would buy him because he has one blue eye and one green, but you, Negrito, who are a sorcerer! You must know that this is good luck! This is wonderful luck! Take him. You may have him!"

The kitten was given me, and I buttoned him inside my jacket, where he set up a steady purring. I hurried back to our apartment as fast as I could, for I knew Mistress would be anxiously awaiting me. She was, standing in the doorway, tapping her foot on the tiles nervously.

"I can't send you out any more, Juanico," she scolded me, annoyed, "if you are going to take so long about my errands!"

"Mistress, I took time to look for a little present for Paquita. And here it is!" I put my hand into my jacket and drew out the little vibrating kitten, with its small pansy face.

"Oh, Mooshi!" cried Mistress, putting it against her neck and nuzzling it. "Thank you, Juanico!" She put the kitten down on the floor, and at once Paquita squealed, and ran for it. The kitten cowered, frightened, and made a little hissing sound. But Mistress fetched a ball of colored wool, and drew it out along the floor, and soon Paquita and Mooshi (for he was never called anything else) were playing happily. Even Niña crowed with delight.

Mooshi became the pet of the household. He kept the little ones entertained, so that they stayed out of Master's studio. Even he sometimes played gravely with the kitten at night, and when Mooshi was grown to a sober, dignified cat, he often sat purring on the arm of Master's chair after supper.

Before that spring turned into summer, the King came one day in state to visit Master and gave him a commission to go and travel in Italy, to see the great works that Rubens had told about, to buy some paintings and sculpture for the palace, and to attend the Infanta Maria in Naples and paint her portrait. The Infanta, sister of the King, was soon to be married to Ferdinand III, King of Hungary.

When Master told Mistress about it, she cried out, "But what about the children? I cannot take them, and I could not bear to leave them behind!"

"I will go alone. With only Juanico," he told her.

Then Mistress cried and stamped her feet and threatened to throw herself out of a window on the fourth floor of the palace. But Master was very patient and soothing, and at last he promised that he would take her and the children to leave them in Seville, with her father, while we were gone.

My preparations were simple. I had only to put a few treasures into a handkerchief and knot it. Master's were not much more complicated, as he wore one suit and carried another. He planned to buy canvases and brushes in Italy.

The King gave orders that our apartment in the palace was to be sealed up and guarded, for our return, and he put a guard on our house in the city, as well. Mistress worried and packed carpets and hangings away, with aromatic herbs, so that moths should not get in to eat them, and hid her silver under a flagstone. At last, weeping and pale, she declared herself ready for the journey, and we set out.

We went in two carriages, Master and Mistress, Paquita and *la niña* ahead; Mistress's maid, cook and I came in the second carriage—a less fancy one, with no springs and no cushions on the seats. But the horses pulled just as steadily, and we always arrived at some inn together at the same hour. One other passenger in our carriage traveled in a box Master had had made for him specially, with breathing holes at the top, and with handles so that I could carry him securely. It was poor Mooshi, who hated the whole journey and mourned constantly inside his box.

My feelings on that journey through Spain were confused. I cannot say, to this day, whether I was happy or not. On the one hand I was grateful to be inside a warm carriage, to be fed hot meals morning and evening, to have bread and wine and fruit when we made a nooning. I was glad to sleep in a warm kitchen, instead of in a drafty stable or under the cold stars. And yet the terrors of that first journey over the same road returned to me, and almost I feared coming upon the grinning gypsy again, with his treacherous smiles and his whip.

At last we saw the golden Giralda of Seville and clattered over a bridge across the flowing brown Guadalquivir. Tears of homesickness then sprang into my eyes, and I remembered everyone I had loved there, from my mother, and old Master and Mistress, to Brother Isidro. I resolved to seek out the little friar, but as things fell out, I did not have time to do so.

There was complete confusion when we arrived at last at the Pacheco house and the tired horses pulled the carriages into the patio. They were unharnessed at once and taken away to be rubbed dry, fed and watered. The rest of us, Master's family and all the Pacheco family and relatives and retainers, became a melee of kissing and weeping and exclaiming, while servants ran about trying to sort out the baggage and get the children to their rooms to bathe and cosset them, and to hear all the news of Madrid and of the court. All this noise and confusion brought on one of Master's headaches. He had them sometimes from sheer nervous exhaustion, when there had been too much excitement, and he went to lie down in the room he and Mistress were to share. I brought cloths wrung out of cold water and gave him one of his pills. Dr. Méndez had made him a pellet of some opium, to deaden the pain and give him rest, when these spells came upon him. Truth to tell, he had never had them before the days when we were so often at court and he was forced to attend so many of the King's ceremonies.

At last Mistress was able to tear herself away from the arms of her father, sisters and cousins, and the old servants who wanted her to bless them, and she came in to look after Master. I went away to see about poor Mooshi, to try to accustom him to this new and strange house. But I need not have worried about him. Paquita had taken him out of his box, brought cold water for him, and a little cream, and then had cuddled up to sleep with him. Entwined in each other's arms, the little girl and the cat sighed in their sleep. I tiptoed away to find out where I was meant to stay. Master Pacheco had laid out covers for me in a corner of his own studio.

While Master was poorly, sick with his headache, and then pale and weak, I could not leave the house, and as soon as he felt better, he said we must start at once, for we were to catch a ship at Barcelona, one of the galleons of the Marques de Spínola. It would be necessary for us to take the first small coastal vessel we could find. I gave up the idea of looking for Brother Isidro, but I asked Mistress to watch out for him and to help him with some oranges or bread, if she could. This was not impertinence; I had done a thousand charitable errands for her always, and I knew her generosity.

When we said our good-bys, I stood aside waiting, while Master embraced and kissed Mistress, and bent down for kisses from his little daughters. I did not expect that a cyclone in baby skirts would throw itself against me, clasping me around the knee and crying, "Juanico not go! Juanico not leave Paquita!" And she would not be comforted. In all my life, no one had ever

wept to see me depart before, and this was an experience I put
away to treasure often in my memory.

I remember little of that first sea journey except my sadness
and nostalgia at the docks, for they put me much in mind of old
Master, who had spent so much of his life at his warehouses
there. After we were aboard our small vessel, I was busy arrang-
ing Master's luggage and making his bed in the tiny cabin. We
sailed with the tide at night, and all was well until we got out
into the open sea. Then I was awakened by Master's groans. He
was most horribly seasick all the way, as the dirty little ship
wallowed and swayed through the water, with respites only
when we put into Málaga and a few other small ports.

At last we arrived in Barcelona, and changed to the large and
splendid galleon of the Marques. Master was pale and frankly
terrified, but this voyage was much less arduous and we passed
it fairly well, though he would take nothing to eat but a little
wine and dry bread. Still, when we arrived in Genoa, we went
first, even before we looked for an inn, to church to give thanks.
I think Master looked upon the sea forever after as an invention
of the devil.

We found a modest inn, but clean. Master made it clear to me
that during our journeys through Italy I was to lie on a pallet in
the same room with him; he did not want me far from his side. I
was glad enough of this, not merely because of the comfort of a
good room, but because I too was lonely. We two, after all, knew
each other's company, and could be silent together for many
hours without feeling any pangs of solitude.

I often went into the inn kitchen to cook for Master because
he was used to a diet of meat and bread, whereas the Italians
ate paste dressed with various spicy sauces, and very little
meat. And when Master felt well enough to go about looking at
art works, visiting galleries and shops, and pricing and bargain-
ing, I went with him, carrying his sketchbook, his clean handkerchief, and his money, which I wore in a sash bound tightly
around my waist.

The Italian cities we visited seemed dirtier and less friendly
than those of Spain, though the people were noisy enough.
There were pickpockets and cutpurses on every side, and I was
often jostled, though they never found anything in my purse but
charcoals bound in a paper, and scrubbing rags. Then the people cursed me, under the breath, and rolled their dark eyes at
me. They were beautiful people, I thought, on the whole, but I
did not understand their language at first, and for some time I

could find no love for them, except inasmuch as they were artists. As Master and I explored the great galleries and visited painters, I grew daily more inarticulate with admiration. Here surely was a country that lived for art and could be pardoned any of its faults.

Master took seats in a carriage for us when we went to Rome. This was a long journey, and while I never initiated conversations with Master, who did not like chatterboxes, we were the only Spanish-speaking travelers, and Master encouraged me to make comments on the scenery as we rolled along.

"The light here is different from that of Spain," he told me. We were being pulled slowly through fields of golden grain where blue flowers and red poppies shone among the sheaves. "Here the light seems liquid and has a soft glow, like firelight. In Spain the light is clear and sharp and blinding. Shadows are deeper, more dramatic, in Spain. Here they are gentle, and they soften the outlines of objects."

I was encouraged to ask, "Do you see this difference of light in the paintings here, Master?"

"I do."

"And will you make copies of paintings in Rome, as you did in Genoa and Florence?"

"Oh, yes. I shall copy some Michelangelo and some Raffaelo and Tintoretto."

"Why do you do this, Master? This copying?"

"Why, the King has ordered some copies. And besides, I learn from them. How better? It is like taking a lesson from a master of the past. I copy his colors, his shadows, his draperies. It is as if he were there, at my shoulder, guiding and teaching me."

I was silent, for I had been struggling with the temptation to buy canvas and colors and a brush, here in this country where nobody knew me, to try to paint by myself. Now the devil added another and stronger temptation. If one could learn by copying, why could I not copy, and learn, also? Master, when he was busy, kept no check on me. I would have time and opportunity.

Where would I get the money for my supplies? Master gave me coins now and then, but there were not enough for such expenses. Well, I sold my earring, the one thing I had that still had been my mother's, that had touched her. So you may judge of the longing I felt to get brush and colors into my hands. And at the first opportunity in Rome, after we had got settled and Master was well into his daily routine, I went and stationed myself in a different gallery from the one where he was working, and got out my bit of stretched canvas and a charcoal stick. I tried to fill in the outlines of a picture which I liked. It was not easy; time and again I rubbed out what I had done with my sleeve and began again. At last the vase and a few squares of tiled floor began to appear on my canvas in proper proportion.

It was wrong, what I was doing, I knew. Worse, I intended to continue it secretly. But my guilty joy was tremendous. It was hard for me to reconcile those two things in my mind. My conscience should have given me no rest. But I gloried in my disobedience and I made occasion to steal from Master's palette, at night when he was asleep, a few little mounds of color. One deception leads inevitably to others.

I had even more opportunity to practice by myself when we went to Naples, for the Infanta was haughty and would not have me in the same room with her when she was being painted.

In this city, while Master was in the great fortress-castle there, with its towers and portcullis, studying and painting the Infanta, I made countless drawings, for I had soon decided that until I could manage the outlines of objects, delineate their shape and their positions in space, there was no point in trying to paint. I burned all those drawings when I had finished them, but I saw how poor and clumsy I was, and I grew discouraged. I became glum and sullen, and Master looked at me sharply a time or two, and once he even scolded me.

"Juanico, I am far from home and lonely, and if you begin to give me dark looks and a long face, I will send you away, for you depress me."

This frightened me and I cried, whereupon he threw up his hands and rolled his eyes heavenward.

"All right, all right, *basta!* I won't send you away, I promise, but do not tempt me. Let me see that bright smile of yours at least, to cheer my day!"

Then I was happy because I had not realized before that he needed my smile, anything of me, but only my services, and to know that I had much to do with his peace and pleasure put warmth into my heart. I even quit my secret drawing for a while.

I do not remember much more of that long time away from Spain. Most of the Italian towns have blurred together and become one in my memory. They were beautiful, with solid buildings, and with beautiful people in the streets, and all were bathed in a golden light. But they were foreign to me, and they did not remain with me, as things seen in a dream do not stay long in the conscious memory. Venice, of course, built along canals of sea water, where the tides rose and fell all day, was different from anywhere else, and it cast an opulent Oriental glow of its own. Here the winter surprised us, and Master had a very bad time with the Italian tailors when he went to order some warm woolen cloaks for us both. First, they wearied him trying to convince him to order a suit in gold and ruby brocade, but he shuddered, as he never wore anything but his sober black. Then they tried flattery, draping a piece of brilliant blue silk against him, to persuade him to have his cloak lined with this, and to hang golden tassels on the edge, to weight it when he wore it thrown back over his shoulder. As the tailors chattered and fluttered their eyebrows at Master and gave him their admiring smiles, I could see what they meant, for in all Italy, which is full of beautiful people, I had not seen a man I considered as fine-looking as he. He was slender and not tall, but finely made, with the delicate hands and ankles and feet of the Spaniard. His face was pale, with thick, upspringing dark hair and well-cut features. His eyes, true, were not as large as those of many of the Italians, but they had a self-contained, observant, sharp look. Somehow I preferred his thoughtfulness, the dignity in his glance and his control to the open emotion of the expression on most Italian faces.

Even the Negroes I saw in Italy (for there were many, both slaves and freed men) were flamboyant and haughty. They were scornful of me, with my plain dark clothes, and my quiet, cool, unpretentious Master. I did not like them.

I was glad indeed when at last we were back in Genoa ready to take ship again. We set ourselves to endure the miseries of the journey, but it was not such a bad crossing, as luck would have it, and Master was not as ill as he had been before. He merely lay on his bunk, pale and apprehensive, and would not eat until our ship tied up at the Seville wharf. Then, even before we got off with our boxes and rugs, he rushed to the dining saloon and ordered a great breakfast of fried eggs and sausages, which he wolfed down in a hurry.

"Do not tell the Señora, Juanico," he said to me, smiling at himself. "I will pretend to nibble at whatever she has ready, with my usual dainty appetite. But I could not wait, having starved myself all the way from Genoa."

He patted his waistline contentedly, took up his rolled canvases and his palette, and I shouldered the rugs. We made arrangements for the rest of our luggage to be sent after us, and we walked through the streets of Seville to Master Pacheco's house.

When we arrived there was a confusion of kisses and cries and embraces. Paquita would not let go of my hand, and Mooshi came and twined around my ankle.

"But where is my *niña*, my Ignacia?" I heard Master's voice ask.

Mistress threw herself into his arms, weeping.

"Ay, Diego, how could I tell you? You were on the high seas . . . it was a month ago . . . and . . ."

He stood perfectly still and quiet, waiting, his eyes never leaving her face, which streamed with tears.

"She . . . our little one . . . our *niña* . . . is dead," she sobbed.

He held her close, patting her heaving shoulders. No one spoke. Master's face looked bewildered, like that of a deaf person who is trying to hear and catches only a few unintelligible words.

Paquita's little voice piped up.

"And I was sick, Juanico, and Niña too. But she didn't get better. She is in heaven now."

I hoisted her to my shoulder. She had always been light, and she was no burden. How I wished I could have had the other little one, to balance on the other shoulder, as in days past.

In silence we went into the house, and the homecoming which was to have been so joyous was shadowed and heavy-hearted.

Master would make no plans to leave. He grieved deeply and went to visit the little grave every day.

And I had another sorrow, too. God had also taken Brother Isidro, who had been so good to me.

But one day a message came from the King, calling us back, and we had to pack our boxes and make ready for the return journey.

It was raining when we left Seville and took the road to the north.

Eight

In which I speak of a small red flower

AS the years went by, Master painted many portraits of court people, but most of the King and his family, and of the King's First Minister, the powerful Duke of Olivares. I would have dis-liked that heavy, hearty-appearing man because of his loud voice and his frequent vulgarity were it not for the fact that he was devoted to Master and never lost an opportunity (even at state banquets) to praise his art. I often reflected, from my own position as servant, that Master, while he had no title of nobil-ity, was far more the gentleman than the wheezing, heavy-drinking Duke, despite his formidable list of titles and honors. Master was always very courteous and noble, a very perfect knight. I had noted growing between Master and the King a very real affection, while, I am sure, Master's feelings toward the for-midable Duke were of caution and reserve.

The King was a quiet man who did not like to speak over-much. This was partly, no doubt, because he had a serious speech defect. He had inherited the long, heavy, out-of-balance jaw of the Hapsburg line, together with their round high fore-head, golden hair and blue eyes. Due to the configuration of his jaw, the King's teeth did not meet squarely, and when he spoke it was with a curious sibilance, as if he were lisping all his words. Besides, I believe that he was shy and that he had learned, in his years at court, that it was fatal to trust anyone with all your heart. So months and years went by, and little by little I could feel his confidence in Master growing, as portrait after portrait came from the studio. The King in black velvet, the King in ceremonial dress, with doublet and trousers all embroi-dered over with silver, the King in hunting gear with his favorite hound and his gun near by.

I was nearly always in the studio when the King was posing; he came to know me as a quiet dark shadow, and paid actually less attention to me than he did to his dog, which he often called to his knee when he sat down to rest between periods of posing. Then he would pull at the velvet ears and scratch the dog under the chin, the animal staring at him with eyes of liquid love. I think the King, for all he was respected and catered to, was not often looked upon with such devotion.

But if the King did not talk much, neither did Master. He kept his own counsel because that was his way, and because, as he once told me, the world is too full of foolish words that had best never been spoken. One time when I was grinding colors, and we were alone in the studio, he told me that he lived by what entered his being through his eyes and by what he gave back from his eyes by means of his painting—not, as other people, by what they took into the mouths and gave back as conversation.

"My canvases are my conversation," he said once to the King. The King thought over this remark and then looked at Master approvingly.

"But then," he asked, after a little time, and I thought sadly, "but then, what is my conversation, Don Diego?"

"Your Majesty was not made by God to converse, but to listen, with affection and paternal care, to his subjects," answered Master. The King liked his words and sat nodding over them, very much pleased.

Between them there grew steadily a silent friendship, and I watched it take shape and grow strong. I am sensitive to shades of feeling between people, and I knew, from month to month and from year to year, how much the King was allowing his hopeful heart to trust in Master's affection. As for Master, he felt a special devotion, almost a tender protectiveness, toward His Majesty, to whom of course he owed so much of all that was important to himself and to his family.

Master painted the King's children with extraordinary delicacy and tenderness, the Infantas Maria Teresa and Margarita, and the little princes Baltasar and Felipe Próspero. Felipe Próspero was sickly, poor little thing, and wailed a great deal, but with Master he was quiet and bright-eyed, and ready to play and to be good and obedient. God took him; he flew to the angels before he was yet four years old.

Of course there were always a few apprentices about, though Cristobal and Alvaro left us after about five years. These took away from Master's shoulders some of the tiresome tasks of painting great expanses of sky or of drapery, and they were often put to copying his religious works because the churches were constantly asking Master for more than he could paint himself.

The apprentices came and went, and Master always taught them conscientiously. What they did not learn, I did, for all those years I kept busy at my drawing, and I had begun, too, to paint, laying on the color as Master did, beginning with a dark underlay, and working up to lighter and more delicate shades for detail.

About fourteen years after our return to Madrid from Italy, a young man came to Master much recommended by the Duke of Olivares. He had been studying painting and wished to apprentice himself to "the greatest in Spain." The young man was about twenty years old, by name Juan Bautista del Mazo. He was rather handsome, vain, and dressed in silk of warm colors; he wore his hair trained into many little ringlets on his brow, such as one sees in Greek statuary.

At that time Paquita was growing up. I had watched her become a lovely young woman, but that first day, after Juan Bautista had joined us, when she came tripping into the studio, swinging her skirts with natural coquetry, I saw our new young man take one look at her and go white. It was a blow of love, as they call it; it had stopped his heart for a moment, draining away his blood. Looking quickly, I saw with new eyes what he had seen, and what I had noticed as a matter of course. She was a young woman in the full bloom of her beauty. She was not tall, but she was rounded and plump as a grape, though with a delicate neck and small waist. She was wearing a dress of golden-brown, fine, soft wool that day, bound with black velvet, and above it her face, with rosy cheeks and sparkling dark eyes, was framed in a little hood. She was going out with her mother and had come in to ask her father for some extra coins with which to buy some frippery. Between those two young people, Paquita and Juan Bautista, there passed an invisible flame; I saw it in her eyes, too, before she swept down her long dark lashes.

"Where are you going?" asked Master, not looking up from his painting.

"To shop and then to visit Angustias."

Angustias was the daughter of one of the court ladies, a great friend of Paquita's. She and Paquita were always visiting each other and giggling over girlish matters and talking about clothes.

"Take Juanico with you. I don't like you to go out without a man along to protect you."

It was quite common for Master to send me along with Paquita or her mother, and they liked to have me go. Paquita loved all small creatures, from babies and birds to little animals; her first Mooshi that I had given her had been succeeded by others, as death or natural cat character, which is independent, had deprived her of her pets. The present Mooshi was a striped tiger with an orange nose, who played roughly, for he was not a gentleman like the white cats from Persia. He was larger and he was fierce, and to show Paquita his love he often seized her hand between his two large paws and pretended to bite her, immediately afterward kissing the place with his rough tongue and purring affectionately. Her little hands sometimes showed his scratches and bites, but she knew his character and she loved him.

She adored plants and flowers, too, and often stopped to caress them and speak to them as if they lived and had personalities of their own. Some of the palace cooks brought her their little pots of herbs to speak to and bless, for they claimed that anything would grow for Paquita.

On that day, I remember, after the visit, we stopped at a flower market and Paquita insisted on buying a little plant in a pot. It was a cold winter day and there were not many plants available; this one, with its tiny four-leaved red flowers, was the only one that showed any blooms.

"Ah, the brave darling, pushing out its little flowers, despite the cold air!" she crooned, and she bent over it and breathed on it. "I must have it!" The flower-seller tried to drive a good bargain, but Paquita's enthusiasm and pretty ways disarmed her, and she let us take away the plant for a few *maravedis*. That plant was to play a curious part in our lives.

The day was not long in coming when Juan Bautista sidled up to me whilst Master was out of the studio for a moment, and asked me to convey a message to Paquita for him.

I shook my head, for I was terrified of family intrigues, and I had heard of slaves having lost their lives for mixing into them. A suddenly outraged father could lose his temper and his head easily enough, and though Master might be deceived, I thought, Mistress was alert and suspicious by nature and nothing escaped her. I refused him, therefore, and took care afterward not to get too close to him, for fear he would strike me or even force a note onto me, which I would have to destroy. I wanted nothing to do with lovers.

However, it was one thing to refuse Juan Bautista and quite another to refuse Paquita. She knew very well that I idolized her and could deny her nothing, and so when she hissed at me from behind a door and signaled me to come to her quietly, my heart sank, for I realized what she wanted even before she held out the little note.

She had folded it into the tiniest possible eight-sided form, and she whispered, "Papá mustn't see you pass this to Juan Bautista, Juanico! I'm depending on you!"

I stood speechless and unhappy with the bit of paper in my hand.

"Don't be so silly about it!" she cried out, angry at me, and stamping her little foot. "There's nothing written on it! There's just a little flower inside. He has seen me watering my plant; he will know what it means!"

I felt less wretched then, for if there were no writing on the paper it was not so dangerous. Anyhow, when I was serving supper that night, I managed to leave it by Juan Bautista's plate. I saw that he slipped it into his sleeve, and with a skill that made me uneasy for our young lady, for it would seem that this gallant had had practice in intrigue.

But, struggle feebly though I had at the beginning, before I knew it I was deep in the lovers' secrecy and part of all their schemes. This worried me and shamed me, but I was like many another who starts an intrigue timidly. Once into it, I had to go on, and therefore I had to harden my sensibilities.

Before long they were meeting for whispered words—two or three—in an out-of-the-way corridor, with me lingering in the background to watch over Paquita and to warn her if I saw anyone coming, or in the King's art galleries, which were, alas, very seldom frequented.

To justify myself I convinced myself that Juan Bautista was really in love with our vivacious Paquita. He toyed with his food and had spells of despondency when he couldn't paint, and he grew thin and pale; these were signs of love that have been celebrated down the ages in poem and song. I might have known Master would have noticed these changes in his best apprentice. But he said nothing.

Paquita, however, became gayer and rosier, more mischievous every day. Her mother watched her nervously, and I saw that Master allowed his eyes to rest on her long and thoughtfully as they sat at dinner.

"Paquita," he said to her one day, "you are growing up very swiftly! We must begin to look around for a husband for you!"

I saw her little gasp of surprise, then an expression of joy, and immediately one of dismay. For Master went on, "I will do a portrait of you and send it to Portugal. It might interest some distant cousins of mine. I should be glad if you made a Portuguese marriage. I am very fond of Portuguese wine."

Master began to peel his orange very calmly, but Juan Bautista dropped his spoon and spent a long time searching about for it under the table, and Paquita kept raising the same glass to her lips and then putting it down again.

"Be in the studio tomorrow at nine o'clock, Paquita, and wear that brown dress. We will begin the portrait."

"Yes, Papá," she whispered, but her eyes were bright and brimming with tears. As for Master, I saw the faintest lift at the corners of his lips, under the dark mustache, and I wondered how much he knew of what had been going on.

Master made a number of his swift sketches and then ordered Paquita to pose in gloves and a little tippet, and to carry her rosary and fan.

Of course she did not pose all day, nor every day either, and to my consternation those lovers redoubled their messages and their meetings. The picture gallery was still their favorite rendezvous, but Paquita was resourceful and clever, and somehow she managed to slip out to many trysts without her mother's knowledge. Often, when they could not meet, I carried the little red flower between them, wrapped in a handkerchief, or pressed into a prayerbook.

As the portrait progressed I could see that Master was holding off painting the face. The features were sketched, the round forehead, the large eyes, the shape of the nose. But he shook his head in a puzzled fashion several times and I saw that he continued to leave it blank, and went on to lavish all his skill on showing the shape of the hand in the glove, the warmth and roundness of the figure under the brown stuff of the dress, even the feather-soft hair . . . but not the spirit and character of the face. I studied her then, as she posed, and I saw what Master had seen and why he held back; there was apprehension in her eyes and a tremor of fear around her lips. He sighed and put away his palette and dismissed her, and went to sit by the window, to stare out at the people passing down below in the courtyard.

I went about my duties, and as I passed toward the kitchen to rinse out some paint rags (Master would not use them when they were stiff with color) Paquita waylaid me and put into my hand a little paper.

"When you can," she whispered to me. "Try to get it to him before Rosary in the chapel."

She fluttered away toward her mother's bedroom, and at that very moment Master appeared in the doorway.

"What have you there, with the paint rags, Juanico?" he asked me, holding out his hand. He must have overheard us.

There was nothing I could do; sick at heart, I handed him her note. He unfolded it, and one of her little red flowers fell out of it, upon the floor. He stooped to pick it up, looked at it most carefully, and then tucked it inside his doublet.

He went back into his studio. I stood hesitating about whether to follow, when he called me. "Juanico! Come here, please."

He was standing at the window, and he had read the note.

"She has misspelled chapel," he said. "Bring me a fine brush and load it with red."

I did so. He took it and corrected the spelling, then he signed a big V to one side, to show that he had read it, and handed it back to me.

"Take it to Juan Bautista," he directed me. "He must be half mad with anxiety, waiting for her. Do they often meet in that art gallery?"

"Yes, Master. Not alone," I hurriedly added, hoping to soften things for Paquita. "I am always there to watch over her."

"The King has asked me to reorganize that gallery," mused Master thoughtfully, "and it is high time I did, if it is always deserted. We can't have all the lovers in the palace trysting there. Oh, give me back that note please, Juanico. There was a little flower in it."

He took the red flower from his doublet, but it was now wilted and sad. He spread out the little velvet petals and studied them. Then he went to get his palette and mixed a thought more white into the red on his brush, until he had exactly matched the shade of the bloom. Then he took the brush, and with four delicate, sure strokes, he put the little flower on paper.

"I could not send the note without its talisman," he murmured. "Take it to Juan Bautista, Juanico. Hold the paper out, the paint isn't dry, and I would not have it smudged. I had an appointment, but I shall cancel it. I feel the need to attend Rosary in the chapel myself today, and perhaps, who knows? I might visit that lonely picture gallery after benediction."

I could not be certain what he was planning and was trembling when I gave Juan Bautista the note. But he knew at once that Master would not withhold his consent, when he saw that V, and Paquita, who knew her father's delicacy of spirit, took heart from the vermilion flower.

I was not with them at Rosary. Master sent me on an errand that took me out of the palace, but that night there was nothing but joy and singing at the table, and the two young people had faces radiant as stars. Master looked calm and self-contained as always. Mistress, though, was crying into her handkerchief and sniffling. There was a dessert of eggs cooked in sherry, something she dearly loved, and usually she took two bowls of it, but on that evening she pushed hers away and would not taste it. Master sat sipping a glass of the wine from Oporto.

"But Juana, my love," he said, "has it been so bad, being married to a painter?"

At those words, she sobbed aloud and cast herself onto his bosom.

"It has been heaven! You know that, my Diego!"

He patted her shoulder and kissed her hair lightly.

"We will allow Paquita a small section of heaven, too," he said, and then it was Paquita who burst into tears and threw herself into his arms on the other side.

"These women will not let me finish my wine," he complained, but he was smiling, and he looked straight into the eyes of Juan Bautista. That young man leaped up and ran around the table to seize Master's hand and kiss it.

The next day Master finished the portrait. He worked swiftly, as he always did when he had fully decided on what he wanted. His brush showed, in each bit of paint he laid on, that young girl's joy and love, her untroubled happiness, her simplicity and her hope. And just under the loop of her sash, placed so as to give the whole composition a little sparkle of color that drew it all together, he painted the small red flower.

Dear Paquita, who was always so kind to me, so lively and merry and gay, who loved little soft and helpless things and God's growing vines and flowers. Paquita, who made me her confidant, so that I might feel some share in the joy of her marriage.

She has lain in her grave now for so many years, but those were very happy days we lived then, and it does my heart good to remember them.

Nine

In which I make friends at court

ABOUT a year after Paquita's wedding I accompanied Master on a trip to the north of Spain with the Royal family. When I learned that we were to make this journey I was much distraught, for I did not know where I could hide the many paintings and drawings I had been making in secret, and I did not want to have to destroy them. There was no one I could trust to care for them, since it was unlawful for me to produce them. As I made ready warm clothes and painting materials for Master's luggage, I was silent and worried until even he spoke to me about it. For, if I have not said so before, I am usually of a happy temperament, and I often hummed or sang as I went about my duties. I had, when I was young, a good bass voice, very deep and strong, and Master liked to hear me singing.

He asked me now why I was so glum and I decided to tell him part of the truth.

"I have a few special treasures to leave," I told him, "and I do not know where I can put them so that they will be safe."

"Is that all? I shall order a box with a lock for you and you may put your things in it and leave it here in my studio, which is always guarded," he told me.

True to his word, he sent a carpenter who had made frames and boxes for us, and he knocked together a strong coffer for me and set on it an iron tongue and hoop, through which I could pass a lock and close it with a key. When I had the opportunity I laid in the box all my treasures—my paintings and drawings (the ones I thought good enough to save), a string of bright green beads which I liked to wear sometimes, a few scarves in brilliant stripes that I had bought in Italy, a small bottle of scent made from jasmine and roses with which I perfumed my hair and hands when I waited on Master or stood behind his chair at some state banquet. I had, too, some women's trinkets I had purchased in Italy with coins Master gave me; I thought I might give them to my wife some day—though Master had never spoken of giving me a wife and I had not forgotten my first love, Miri. I had never looked with eyes of love on any other girl.

I disliked the whole thought of this journey we were to make, for it was a hunting excursion, and we had accompanied the King on similar trips before. The King was very fond of hunting, and I knew that every day they would be bringing back deer, pheasants and hares; the thought made me ill. I could not bear to hurt anything, not even a mouse, and cannot to this day. Cook had long since ceased calling me into the kitchen to bash the little scurrying creatures as they ran across the shelves, for I would never do it, and once I had found and tried to save five tiny newborn pink baby mice I found in a sack of dried corn. I struggled to nurse them to health with warm milk and water, but in that I was unsuccessful and had to bury the little tender corpses. I trembled now at the thought of the banging and shooting, the cries of the hares, the bloody feathers, the wounded deer.

But Master had said I was to accompany him and I had no choice. I could not even feign illness; I was never sick.

He himself was not a hunter, and I had never seen a gun in his delicate hands. He had it in mind to make some portraits of the King in hunting dress and on his charger in the forests, and so I ground all the earth colors he might want, as well as green and ochre.

Mistress would not go, though His Majesty had cordially offered to have a special tent set up for her, with every comfort. Paquita was delicate, expecting her first child, and she would not leave her.

I endured what I must, waiting with Master in shelters of boughs in the forest while the King thundered past on his great hunting steeds, passing Master the colors and brushes he needed for his swift sketches, and later piling the stiff, bloody creatures of the hunt into compositions, of which Master painted a good many.

He looked at me sharply once, for he saw that my face was streaming with tears as I moved a deer from whose muzzle there still dribbled a little stream of blood, and a soft hare, its long ears so daintily marked with tiny red branching veins.

"You hate this so much?" Master asked, wonderingly.

"God gave these creatures life, and it wounds me to see it torn from them so violently."

"But you eat meat at table, Juanico."

"I know it. I am ashamed, but I do."

"You are a gentle creature," he mused. "You must have come of very admirable people."

"My mother was lovely and good."

"Yes, my aunt told me."

But my loyalty to Master was strong and I could not allow him to exclude himself from tender and compassionate people just because he was not moved by the dead creatures of the chase.

"You are good also, Master, and most kind," I protested passionately, "even if you paint these animals without any emotion."

"Ah, but I do feel emotion, strong emotion," he told me, looking with fierce intentness at the wound in a deer's throat. "But my emotion is the detached emotion of a spirit or an angel, something not of this earth. Painters are like this, I think; they train themselves to be so. We must represent the essence of what we see, with no extra strokes. Personal human emotion dare not enter in, for then the hand would tremble and one would be tempted to drop soft veils over anything painful or repulsive."

"In Italy," I began shyly, for I loved having him talk to me like this, "I heard the painters talking in the galleries, and they were saying that all that is not beautiful should be subdued or hidden."

"I am more humble than they," he answered me, "for I do not wish to try to improve upon the works of God I merely show, with respect, what He has made."

One day as the King came by, gun in hand, followed by his hound, I said, "Corso looks sad. Is he sick?"

Naturally I could not address the King, who pretended not to have heard me, but Master repeated my words, adding, "I think the dog does look dejected, Majesty. Is he off his feed?"

"Well yes, he is, I am afraid," the King answered worriedly, stopping to lean down and pat the dog's head. "I offered him some tidbits at breakfast, and he took them in his mouth but then he threw them down without eating."

"My servant, Juanico here, is good at curing house animals," said Master. "If your Majesty so orders, I will have him dose Corso."

The King stood still, taking time to think things over; he always did this. He was a most cautious and careful monarch. Then he looked at me with his thoughtful light blue eyes.

"I am willing that this slave of yours should try," he pronounced at last. And he motioned me to come nearer so that I might examine the hound.

I had often dosed Mistress's little dogs, for they were always fed too much meat and bread and this was too heavy for them, animals that by rights should have run in the fields to exercise and there eaten the herbs they needed.

"I must open the hound's mouth," I said to Master, and he repeated it.

"Corso," ordered the King (for the dog would obey no one but him), "stand quiet."

I touched the dog's head which should have felt silky but instead seemed dry and coarse, while it looked at me with big suspicious eyes. I then gently opened the jaws and put my head down to sniff the dog's breath. It had a strong metallic odor. This confused me. I also reflected that Corso had plenty of exercise and could have stopped anywhere around the King's camp to swallow the grasses these animals eat to purge themselves.

The strange smell on Corso's breath and the slight film I saw on what should have been clean and shining white fangs made me suspect something else, and I gingerly felt along the dog's flank until it gave a sudden yelp of pain and then crouched trembling against the King's leg. His Majesty petted Corso and tried to comfort him.

"I think this hound has a sick liver," I told Master. "He may have a parasite encysted there."

The result was that Corso was turned over to me and I looked after him—not without trepidation, for it had occurred to me that if I failed and if the hound should die, His Majesty's wrath might be directed against me. But God was with me, for in the fields around about I found herbs to brew a draught that shocked the animal's liver into strong action, and after two days he expelled the parasite. Thereafter he got better at once and began to frisk about and to eat ravenously again. At the end of a week I was able to take Corso back to the King's hunting tents, lively and merry. Corso fawned against me and ran to the King and then back to me, giving first His Majesty and then me, the humble slave, little loving butts with his head and doggy kisses. I saw His Majesty's very rare and very sweet smile.

"I thank you," he said simply, and he held out to me a velvet bag full of ducats.

Master was very proud of me and would not take the money, which of course was rightfully his, since slaves are not allowed to own property.

"No, put the ducats in your strong box," he told me. "Buy yourself something. An amethyst ring, perhaps."

Master loved to look at jewels and often studied them in various lights, although he never wore any. Nothing was too wonderful or too terrible, for his eyes. But he did not care to adorn himself, and never did.

Back in the palace, after the hunting, Master's interest turned to those strong and often pitiful creatures the King kept about to entertain his family and the court. There were a few clever old actors, who told jokes and played parts in different costumes. Master often asked their services in modeling historical or mythical personages, and the actors took pride in finding the right stance and the most suggestive expression for these pictures.

Also there were always several dwarves and one or two gentle idiots whose constant laughter seemed to please His Majesty. He looked after all these entertainers very well, gave them good and warm clothing and plenty to eat and drink. For the dwarves he had tailors make special suits, and the shoemakers little boots to fit the misshapen feet.

As Master painted all these court entertainers at various times, I became well acquainted with all of them. The idiot boy called "El Bobo" could not talk sensibly and he laughed almost all the time, but he was kindly, poor soul, and everyone in the palace treated him affectionately. He was one of God's innocents, as they say, and the little Prince Baltasar Carlos loved to be carried in his arms and clung to him trustingly. Master painted El Bobo and also the little dwarf El Niño de Vallecas, who was the constant companion of the boy-prince, being a man, but no taller than Baltasar Carlos when he was three.

This dwarf, the Niño de Vallecas (his real name was Francisco Lezcano), had been found in the country and brought to the court, for the King was constantly searching for such little beings. He was greatly deformed in body, very twisted, and he suffered intermittent pain. I often gave him massages to try to soften and slacken the tense muscles of his crooked legs and of his humped back. He was not overly intelligent—I think his suffering drove learning from his mind—but we became friends and he lived for seven or eight years in the palace before he died.

"We are brothers," he used to say to me in his strange, deep voice like a man's, "you and I, because we are enslaved by reason of the way we were born. You were born strong, a fine normal being, but black. I was born as I am, a man in the body of a little creeping child. Why did God put this burden on us, Juanico?"

"To make us humble, maybe. Our Lord was despised and rejected, you remember. He himself told us so. And He said, 'He who exalts himself shall be brought low, and he who humbles himself shall be lifted up.'"

72

"Be careful what you say. It might be thought treason. Our King is very high."

"He was born to his station, but he is a gentle person who speaks to me in the corridors, and who sometimes touches me kindly."

"My poor Juanico, you are satisfied with very little."

"Not so. But I am a guilty man. That is why I try not to be rebellious against the state of life I was born to."

And . . . I marvel at it now . . . but I suppose my secret had been preying on my conscience for so long that I had to tell someone. . . . I told the Niño de Vallecas about my passion for art and my longing to paint. He listened to me and smiled at me with great pity, and then all he did was pat my hand with his own little gnarled fingers. Nevertheless, I felt comforted.

Master painted him laughing, but in that carefree expression he revealed, ironically, all the tragedy of the dwarf's life.

There were other dwarves in the court also. One was a little bearded man not three feet tall, with the tough, wily face of a campaign soldier, and there was another one, gentle and pale, who was actually in charge of the books in the chancellery. This last was somehow the most pitiable of them all, for he had the face of an intellectual, and his deep-set, sad eyes were brilliantly intelligent. Yet he had a small, wizened body, and the hands that turned the leaves of the great books were no larger than those of the baby prince. He was called Diego de Acedo, although the King sometimes jovially addressed him as Cousin. I wondered why, sometimes. Was it because both were pale and sad-eyed? Or because they both loved books and figures? Or maybe poor Diego was really some sort of relative. Noble families were not likely to be proud of a misshapen child, and they had ways of hiding them or of foisting them off on poor families who were glad to get the money to care for such unwanted little creatures. Well, I will never know about this, as I will go to my grave not knowing many other things that have preoccupied my mind.

For some time I resented the meticulous way Master painted these deformed and pathetic beings. He was making obeisance to the truth as he saw it. He had explained that to me often enough. And yet it seemed to me cold-blooded, even cruel. But later, when I looked at those portraits years after, I saw what he had done, and what glossing over their deformities could not have achieved. He had painted, in every case, a soul imprisoned.

Ten

In which I confess

OUR apprentices came and went. Master never sought them, but often he felt obliged to take in some stripling whose father, some courtier, or a friend, asked it.

In those later years, after Paquita was married, the studio was a quiet, even a somber place, for Master took no apprentices at all for two or three years. Such apprentices as he felt obliged to consider, he sent over to Juan Bautista, Paquita's husband, no doubt thinking that the young people could use the money, such as it was, that apprentices brought in from the fees they paid for learning, or by sales of copies they made of pictures done by their Master. Also he felt that Paquita, with her new baby girl, should have the help and the companionship of young people around her. She had had a hard birth and had not been well since, and was much inclined to tears and despondency.

Then one day a young man came riding into our courtyard on a heavily laden mule. He was dressed simply in a white shirt and woolen knee-trousers, and he wore cheap cloth shoes on his feet, laced on around the ankles. Lashed onto the mule's back was a bundle of clothes, a rug, a guitar, and painting gear.

"Hola!" he called up to where I looked down on him from our second-story windows. "I have come to pay my respects to Maestro Velázquez!"

I hurried down the stairs to ask him his business, and by the time I arrived in the patio he had begun to unload his mule, singing a merry song meanwhile. I stopped in my tracks. It was wonderful to hear that lighthearted caroling, and I realized how sad and silent our household had become, with Paquita gone, and Mistress spending half her time in her daughter's house, trying to build her up and lift her spirits.

"I am Juan de Pareja, Master's servant," I told him. "Before you unload, we had better find out if you can stay."

"Oh, I'll stay!" cried the young man confidently. "I have letters from old friends of his in Seville. And besides, even if I am turned away, you must let me rest my animal. Poor old Rata!" He petted the dejected mule's nose. "He has come a long way and he is tired!"

I could hardly resist his kindness to the animal; that was always a way into my soft heart.

"I will go and ask if Master can speak to you," I told him. "Who is calling on him?"

"Bartolomé Esteban Murillo. From Seville. And I have come to be his apprentice and to learn from him because he is the best in the world!"

He was stocky and broad, with a round dark face and undistinguished features save for the fine brown eyes. They were full and lively, and sparkling with kindness and good humor. His hair, roughened by the autumn breeze, was a dark chestnut brown, curly and worn rather long, though not as an affectation, I am sure, but only because he had no money to cut it. On his brown chest, showing in the open throat of his travel-stained shirt, lay a crucifix, suspended from a black leather cord.

"Lead on, Señor Pareja," said the young man. "I want to feast these eyes on the finest painter who ever lived!"

Now I had never been called Señor Pareja in my life. Slaves are not addressed in this way. It showed the young man's ignorance, or perhaps merely his preoccupation. I did not say anything; he would soon learn. Everyone called me Juanico.

"If you have letters, Master will want to see you at once," I told him. "Follow me."

The young man patted his bulging sash, to make sure his letters were still safe, and came trotting along behind me. But he turned and said, "First, could I get some water for my mule? Poor fellow, he's thirsty."

I went to draw a bucketful myself. It gave me time to think over young Sr. Murillo from Seville. I began to hope that Master would accept this simple young man, for I liked him well.

After old Rata had sunk his nose in the bucket of water and I had found him some fodder, Bartolomé tethered him in the shade. Then he laid a light blanket over him. Only after all this had been done, did he turn, ready to follow me into Master's studio.

That day Master had begun to work out an idea for painting several people in the same room by reflecting them in mirrors. He was busy placing mirrors here and there, checking their positions, going to his easel to observe the proportions of the images reflected and sketching a few lines. He was not satisfied and had begun to rub out some of his charcoal lines with a clean white rag when we reached the door.

Bartolomé ran forward, dropped on one knee, seized Master's hand still holding the paint rag, and pressed it to his lips.

"Bartolomé Esteban Murillo," he announced himself. I saw that his dark eyes were glittering with tears of emotion. Master looked at the kneeling young man without expression; I had no clue as to what he was thinking.

"You have got charcoal dust on your face," he said then. "Get up, young fellow. One should kneel and kiss hands only to the King. What brings you here?"

Wordless, Bartolomé got to his feet and took two letters from his sash, which he gave to Master. Master carefully wiped his hands clean and then went to sit in his big chair near the window. He opened and read his letters.

"It is good to have news of old friends," he said, turning. "So you are a painter, Murillo?"

Bartolomé crossed himself in the most natural manner and answered, "With the grace of God, I sometimes do pretty well. But I have much to learn, and I want to work in your studio."

"Did you bring some of your work to show me?"

"I did!" And without another word, Bartolomé flew down the stairs to where he had left the load of luggage beside his mule. In a couple of minutes he was back again with several rolls of canvas. Instinctively choosing the right place to stand so as to show his painting in a good light, he unrolled his canvases, one by one.

Master studied each one in silence.

"You paint saints and angels," he said, in his customary, dry, serious tone. "But you paint from live models."

Bartolomé stepped forward smiling, eager to explain.

"Christ is in each one of us," he explained. "When I need to paint a saint, I find holiness in the face of anyone available. It is always there. As for angels, I use little children! There is so little difference between an angel and a child!"

Master studied his face, and then I saw one of his rare, slow smiles move his lips slightly and light up his deep-set eyes.

"Juanico, help Murillo bring up his things and give him the small room next to yours."

"Maestro!" Bartolomé stepped forward impetuously, as if about to seize Master's hand again, but Master quickly put it behind his back and laughed out loud.

"Control yourself, Murillo! I am not used to such open adulation. You will turn my head!"

"Oh, forgive me. It is only that I am so happy!"

And so he came to live with us and to bring laughter and singing and joy back into our quiet studio.

Murillo's jokes all day and his songs to the guitar after supper brought Mistress much joy, and when he was in the studio

he was an indefatigable painter. At first Master set him to copying some of his own religious works, for there were always orders coming in from churches and convents and he could never
keep up with them. Then, little by little, he simply let Bartolomé
paint along at his side, Master suggesting and correcting, and
Bartolomé listening and learning. Master began bringing in
models once more, especially street children (that Mistress fed
and coddled in the kitchen) and old men, to whom Mistress gave
warm cloaks and odds and ends of clothing. Master painted the
men in the guise of great personages of the past or dressed as
saints and holy people. Murillo saw the Christ-light in each one,
but Master's interest was in what these people represented indi-
vidually, in what made them different from everyone else. In
that way, he found his truth.

Now I must confess that in that happy, tranquil time, with
Mistress presiding over dinner and supper, Master working all
day by the side of Bartolomé, and Paquita coming often to visit,
with her little plump dark-eyed daughter, in that time I returned
with passion to my secret vice, painting. I used the ducats the
King had given me to buy canvases and brushes and, God help
me, I stole colors constantly. I kept on because it seemed to me
that at last I was beginning to progress in that difficult, demanding art. Why should I not? I also worked by the side of the
greatest Master in the world, though my work was invisible to
him. And Murillo, too, though he painted in another way from
Master, being softer and more sentimental generally, was worth
learning from. I copied them carefully and began to make my
own direct studies of color, and of light and shade, and perspec-
tive. Everyone in that household was busy and happy, and
therefore they were not alert to suspicion. I had many hours to
myself. This is what gnawed at my conscience and made me unhappy all the while—that Master trusted me.

Especially did I feel sick with repentance when I went with
Murillo to early Mass. He was a daily communicant, and I often
marveled, as I watched him lift that round, earthy, commonplace face with closed eyes to receive the Host, how God laid a
light of sanctity around his ordinary features at that time. And
I? Unable to promise that I would stop deceiving Master, steal-
ing his colors, and painting by myself . . . I could not confess
and be absolved. Shamed, guilty, I knelt, but I could not receive
the grace, and therefore Murillo, good soul, began to worry
about me.

"Juan, my friend," he used to say, "go to confession! Cleanse your soul so that you may receive the Eucharist once more! There is no earthly joy to compare with it!"

He never called me Juanico, as everyone else did. On Master's lips, and Mistress's, and even Paquita's, "Juanico" sounded good to me, sounded affectionate and intimate and kind. But I hated it when other men addressed me so, for they were giving me careless treatment, as they might a dog. And yet, being a slave, I could not expect to be called "Señor Pareja." I braced myself each time some stranger snapped his fingers at me and called me "Juanico," and the years never softened my resentment. As often as I could, I pretended not to hear. I loved Bartolomé for finding, in his kindness, the right way to address me. "Juan, my friend."

"Juan *amigo*," he said, "if I can help you, let me."

"I will think things over," I promised him.

And I thought. I wrestled with my problem. But I could not bring myself to speak of it to him, nor yet to confess. And this was a torture, for at any time I might be taken ill, or have some accident, and if I died I would have to appear before the Judgment Seat with all my sins on my head, unconfessed, unrepentant, and unpurged.

I was then trying, hidden in my room, to paint a Virgin. Such temerity had I. But I felt an overpowering need to represent on canvas the tender, youthful face of Our Lady at the moment when the angel appeared to her and said, "Hail, full of grace! Blessed art Thou amongst women!" and told her that she was to be the mother of God.

I had stretched a good piece of Holland linen, which had cost me dear, and I had drawn in the figure, full length, with folded hands. The eyes were downcast and the face was gravely serious, as would become a maiden being told such transcendental news. All the proportions were true. All was ready for the laying on of the color. I had labored over that drawing for many hours.

At last I was ready to begin stroking on the color. I had ready two brushes, one delicate and fine, made of squirrel hair, and another coarser, heavier, for strong strokes.

I began. I had been careful in sketching the garments—the way the skirt molded itself around the young limbs, the folds in the long sleeves, the way the cloak clung around the hair and opened softly over the high-necked bodice of the dress. I worked happily, and it seemed to me that I had caught at last Master's way of laying on a tiny sparkle of light where the material folded, and a soft depth of shadow where it fell away.

A few days later I began to paint the face. First I stroked on the undercolor, in deep earthy rose, as Master always did, then bringing up the colors, layer on layer, until the flesh tones were perfect, reflecting the life and light, suggesting the fullness of flesh and veins and beating blood beneath the warm skin. As I painted, working up the colors on the bit of broken porcelain I used for a palette, some changes began to take place. My hand made those changes while my eyes watched in wonder, as if I had no control over myself at all. The face of the Virgin I was painting became subtly darker, the features softer and more round. The face was becoming that of a girl of my own race, the eyes enormous, velvety black, faintly showing the sparkling white around them, the nose broad with sensitive, flaring nostrils, the lips fleshy, with deep corners. The hair, where it showed beneath the hood of her cloak, was black, tightly curling. I had painted a Negro madonna.

At first I was satisfied, even happy with my painting. Then I felt sorrow, for it seemed as if some devil had guided my hand and that I had painted Our Lady as a Negro maid in order to exalt myself and to protest that my race was the chosen one. I put my head into my hands and wept.

Then I thought, Could it be that an angel had guided me to paint in this manner so as to make me realize fully how wrong it was to try secretly to put myself on the same plane as Master, to show him that I could be as good as he was, could paint as well, could reveal my race in beauty, just as he showed the dignity, the pride of the Spaniard? I was all confused and I did not know what to do, and so I wept and suffered great torment of soul.

Until I remembered the kindness of Bartolomé and that he always called me Friend.

One day, not long after I had finished my painting and before it was yet dry, Master came down with one of his crippling headaches. I did all I could for him with massages, cold cloths on his neck, and teas to induce sleep, and when at last he was dozing fitfully and would be better, I knew, I darkened his room and crept out. Mistress came to sit beside Master, and I was quite free for a few hours. The decision, sudden and final, came into my mind to ask Bartolomé's help. I went to find him in the studio, where he was working on a very large canvas covered with angels and clouds.

"Bartolomé, I need you. Come with me," I begged him simply, and he at once put down his palette, cleaned his hands, and prepared to follow me. I led him to my little room and closed the door behind us. As soon as his eyes had become accustomed to the semi-dark, he saw my painting.

He cautiously stole over to open the door slightly so that he could get good light on my picture, and so he studied it for a good twenty minutes. Then he turned it gently against the wall, and shut the door.

"Let us go out where we can talk freely," he said, and telling the cook that we would be back in about an hour, in case Master wakened and asked for either one of us, we left. Outside, as if in perfect accord, we took the street that led to a little church where we often attended Mass together.

Looking around to make sure that no one would overhear us, Bartolomé then clasped my hand and said, "It is a fine painting, *amigo*. I congratulate you! You handled the figure, the draperies, the light with all the skill of a pupil of Maestro Velázquez! But what troubles you so?"

"It is unlawful for me, a slave, to paint," I told him.

At this news his jaw dropped and he looked upset and bewildered. "But how can that be?" he protested.

"It is the law in Spain. Slaves may be artisans or craftsmen, but they may not practice any of the arts. That is why I have been painting in secret. I have been copying Master's work for years, and practicing drawing. Alone."

"I am a stupid fellow," said Bartolomé, "and never see beyond the end of my nose. I may have heard of this law, but I cannot remember. I am poor; my family never had slaves. But, Juan, if you have never offered any competition to free men, how can it be thought that you have broken the law?"

In his simplicity, he saw intent as the very essence of the law and could not accept the idea that I had been at fault.

"And you have studied well," he went on. "I myself would be proud to sign the canvas you have just shown me."

"You are always kind. But, you see, that is why I cannot confess. The priest would ask me to give it up, and I cannot! I cannot!"

"Now wait," said Bartolomé. "Wait a moment. Let us think this matter over quietly. Is it a *sin*, then, to paint? I have never heard so."

"But I am a slave!"

"Is it a sin, then, to be a slave?"

"No. It is an injustice. But I am a religious man. I do not expect justice here on earth, but only in heaven. And I am not a rebellious slave. I love Master and Mistress."

"You are a good man. And I cannot see that you have done any wrong. When you confess, does the priest ask you your status? Does he say, 'Are you a slave?' or 'Are you a sinner?'"

"He never asks. I only say that I am a sinner. That I have sinned." I saw what he was driving at and I began to feel the most exquisite pang of hope.

"I cannot see that you are obliged to confess your painting, my friend," said Bartolomé, "and mind you, I am very scrupulous. Painting is no sin and it has nothing to do with your receiving the Host."

"But I have stolen colors."

"Well then, you must confess that and promise to do it no more. You won't have to, for I will give them to you. Now where is the problem? Let us go and find a confessor this very moment."

We went quickly toward the little church and took our places in the line of folk who had gone to confess. Bartolomé, as was his custom, fell almost at once into ecstatic prayer. As for me, I confided in him absolutely. Because I wanted to believe what he told me, of course. That was part of it, I know now. But also because it had been made clear to me in my mind that he was right.

At last my turn came, and I confessed. I told of angers I had felt, of times when I had been slothful, of having stolen little mounds of color. I told of the worst sin, that I had despaired of the love of God, and that I had, in my pride, supposed that God's mercy and forgiveness, which are boundless, would be withheld from me.

The priest gave me a stern penance and I rose from my knees and went to kneel once more beside Bartolomé. He could not know, ever, what a gift he had made me, by making me see that I could be shriven and could once again receive Our Lord. I vowed in my heart that I would serve him as faithfully as I served Master in whatever time I had free.

As we strolled home he said in his simple way, his countenance all radiant with joy, "Now you can be a communicant again, Juan my friend! I rejoice for you!"

"I wish I could show my painting to Master!" I cried then. I had a great longing for his eyes to rest on my work.

Bartolomé's face changed swiftly, and peasant prudence showed in it.

"If you wish my advice, do not show it. Not just yet. The time will come. . . . You will realize when the hour has struck that you should show it, and let him know what you have been doing. Not yet. . . ."

"Do you think it was a mistake to paint Our Lady as a Negro girl?" I asked, humbly.

"How so?" asked Bartolomé. "Our Lord appears in many forms to loving Christian souls. As a child, as an old man, sometimes even as a leper. And Our Lady can reveal herself within the body of a child, of an Italian girl, a Spanish maid, or a young woman of the black race. Her tenderness, her gentleness, her sanctity can shine through whatever vessel she chooses to house her spirit for a time. And," he turned to me and laid his hand on my arm in affection, "and the gentle women of your race, Juan, have a beauty Our Lady would never scorn."

So we returned, and my life from that moment grew broader and happier and I became a better person, I think, for Bartolomé had turned my mind away from small preoccupations, and led it into paths of Truth. I stole no more colors. He gave them to me, and he gave me brushes and canvas also.

I served Master and Mistress and Bartolomé and I painted. I felt that life could offer me no further joys.

Eleven

In which I return to Italy

BARTOLOMÉ was with us three years and then he went back to Seville. He used to write to us sometimes. He married there, and had a large studio with many apprentices, and he did countless commissions on religious themes for the Church. I often thought of him and wished him well with all my heart, and I sent my love to him over the miles between us.

In the year 1649 His Majesty gave Master a commission to go to Italy to collect paintings and statuary for the palace and for museums. There were many preparations for this journey, and toward the end, just before our departure, we had to make some sudden changes in plan. Master had wanted to sail from Seville, but there was pest there and it was thought better not to risk the danger. Barcelona was then in the hands of the French. So, in the end, we made the journey overland to Málaga and took ship there.

It was a cold winter day early in January, and a misty rain was falling as we went aboard. Poor Master began to look pale and apprehensive the moment we stepped on deck, as it lifted gently beneath his feet. He was remembering his illness on our first journey, and alas! he had reason to be fearful of the immediate future. We passed the most horrible forty days of my life, or his, on the water.

Shortly after we left port we ran into a fierce storm, and so roughly were we thrown about that we had to lash ourselves into our bunks and simply endure the heaving and straining and wallowing of the ship. It was terrifying beyond compare, and the screeching of the sails and groaning of the timbers gave the impression that at any moment the ship might simply give up struggling and go down to the bottom. Even I could not lift my hand to wait on Master, being sick and weak as a drowned kitten myself, and there we lay, unwashed, miserable and untended for three days and nights, until the worst of the storm had passed. But even then the water was rough and the waves were tall. When Master arose and tried to stagger across the cabin to get clean clothes from his box, he was thrown against the bulkhead and he badly cut and bruised his right hand.

I took care of him as best I could. I washed him and helped him change, and I put aromatic oils on his hand and bandaged it. But long before we came into Genoa, the hand was swollen and most painful, and poor Master did nothing but lie on his bunk, cradling it in his left hand, trying not to cry aloud. I watched carefully, and as the hand did not show those dangerous marks in red along the vein, which meant great danger, I had hopes it would get better in time.

After we had landed in Genoa, we went straightaway to find a barber-surgeon, who pressed and felt the injured hand until Master fainted. Before he came to himself, I simply picked him up and heaved him over my shoulder and carried him away; I was deadly frightened that the barber would want to open Master's hand with a knife and let out the bad blood. It seemed to me that it would be better to cure the hand myself with hot packs and herbs, and save it without scars for Master. After all, that hand of his was more valuable than all the city of Genoa put together.

And so I took him away and carried him to a comfortable inn in the city. I kept soothing leaves and hot cloths bound around his hand for twenty-four hours of every day, meanwhile ordering plenty of strong hot soup and sweet gruel and red wine for Master to take to keep up his strength and cleanse the blood. Thank God I was guided aright, and the swelling went down, the angry scratches closed with a sound scab, and the hand ceased to throb.

"You shall ask what you wish of this hand, Juanico," breathed Master on the morning when he saw it returned to its proper shape and color at last, "and I will give it to you."

I thought of many things, but it seemed to me that it would be wrong to demand payment for what had been an act of true devotion on my part. Besides, whenever I had need of anything important that Master could give me, I had only to mention it, and he did. So I said, "Master, I ask nothing. I might some day, but just now there is nothing in the world I want more than your own good health. I give thanks to God that your hand is saved to paint hundreds more glorious pictures!"

He said nothing, for he was always a silent man, but I could see that he was storing up my words in his memory.

In Genoa, when he was entirely well, he visited many galleries and collections and chose several paintings for the King, which he arranged to have sent back on a Spanish galleon. Then we began a journey overland toward Venice. Towns in Italy, unlike Spain, were often very close together, an easy day's walk, and when the weather was fine we frequently set out in the dewy morning with a loaf of bread and some cheese and wine, sending our boxes and rugs along by mule. Master had been warned that this was foolhardy, as there were many thieves abroad, but he replied that we carried nothing of value, and as to food, he would gladly share it with any traveler who was hungry. Actually we were never bothered, nor even made suspicious, and the country folk were kind and hospitable. Much more so than the city people, who were often sly and, seeing that we were foreigners, tried to cheat us in some way. We never carried purses anyhow, and Master and I both kept a few coins in sashes bound about our waists and in our shoes. The King's bankers had arranged for moneylenders to have sums ready for us upon our arrival in Venice and in Rome.

What we did carry were a few stretched canvases, charcoal, and colors. Often Master wanted to set down the light that fell, cut into delicate patterns, through an avenue of leafless trees, or the glisten of dew on a bog, or the shine of a stream as it ran between brown fields. It was winter and it was cold. A sudden snowstorm caused us to remain several days in an old town, Cremona by name, where Master amused himself by searching out a family of renowned makers of violins. He had heard about them and their instruments from travelers who spoke about the tradition of woodworking and of secret varnishes these families had kept to themselves through generations.

Another time we were caught on the roads by a storm of sleet and wind, and Master was chilled to the bone. This brought on sharp pains in his hand, and once again it swelled to twice its size and was feverish. When we came to an inn, Master would not stir from his room and I could see that he was becoming very frightened. And why not? His hand had been his livelihood since he was young; in it was all the knowledge, all the skill, all the art he had learned in almost thirty years of steady labor.

I did all I could for him and tried to persuade him to call in one of the skillful Italian surgeons, but he would not, as he had a mortal fear of them. I was at my wit's end, and Master would not speak at all but lay in a kind of despairing stupor. There was nothing to do but pray.

So I left him, warmly covered, and went out to find the main church of that town. I threw myself on my knees before the image of the Virgin and wept. I had been infected with Master's fear for his hand, and I could not bear it. I implored her help, and I promised that if she would turn her eyes in mercy on Master and heal him, I would confess my wickedness in painting secretly and make all amends and bear all punishments, on our return to Spain.

Whether it was my tears, blurring my sight, or some trick of the winter light coming in from a very high window, or whether it was indeed a miracle I do not know. But it seemed to me as I begged the Virgin for this favor that she smiled at me and inclined her head slightly toward me, in assent. Anyway, I took it for a sign to hope, and I was greatly comforted. I remained to pray a whole Rosary, with the greatest fervor and love, and then I hurried back to the inn where poor Master lay in his misery and despondency.

When I entered the room, I saw that the fire had died down and it was growing cold. I called for more wood and built up good leaping flames, and drew the curtains, then I went down to the kitchen to order a pot of strong broth and some grilled meat for him to eat. When I returned, Master had not moved on his couch, and I went to touch him. He was cool; there was a light beading of sweat on his brow, and he was breathing steadily and deeply.

As I stood there, he moved, changing position as a person does who is sleeping healthily, and sighed deeply. He thrust out the injured hand, and it lay against the dark coverlid white and delicate and nervous, the puffiness and redness gone. Even the scratches and scars had disappeared, and not an hour ago I had left it looking poisoned, doomed. It was his hand, his marvelously trained and skillful hand, as it had always been. I fell on my knees by the bed and took that hand and kissed it.

Master woke and sat up.

"Juanico!" Master looked at me there on my knees. "What has happened?"

"Your hand, Master!"

He lifted it, flexed it, and then laughed aloud.

"Oh, thanks be to God!" he cried, and I echoed, "Amen."

He got up then and ate a hearty supper.

The next day we journeyed on to Venice, but in a hired carriage, and Master, who never sang, hummed most of the way under his breath, or pursed his lips and whistled softly.

I remembered Venice well, and the peculiar light that prevails there, different from that of the rest of Italy. In most parts of the country the sunlight is softly golden, but in Venice it has a pale blue tinge, a radiant pure light, rather cold, a kind of reflection from the sea.

Master had begun to paint again, as well as carry out his many commissions. But the whole frightening time with the pain and fear of losing his hand, which was the quintessence of all his worth, had affected him in his soul. Now he was nervous about his drawing and greatly upset when he began to lay color on the canvas. Sometimes his brush trembled slightly in his fingers, and this was enough to throw him into a black mood and into silence for hours. He began to worry about his ability to do portraiture any more. And this had always been the foundation and mainstay of his art.

He started a portrait of a Venetian lady, but he was most displeased with it, and suddenly gave her back the advance ducats she had paid him and told her he could not continue. He destroyed the canvas and that very night he arranged for us to have seats in a carriage for Rome the next day. We were several days going, and though Master stared at the changing countryside, which was beautiful, for spring had come and was dressing all the leaves and vines in new green leaves, he sat all the while holding his right hand in his left and stroking and massaging it.

"There is a tingling in the fingers. I don't like it, Juanico," he confessed to me. "What will I do if I can never paint again?"

"God would not have tormented you with the pain and trouble if He were not planning your reward," I assured him staunchly. Master smiled his small ironical smile. "Let us trust that He means to send the reward while I am still on earth. Otherwise, we shall starve, Juanico."

"I have no anxieties about that, or about your painting, Master."

"My loyal Juanico. I could not do without you."

When we arrived at last in Rome, we went to one of the best inns in the city, but we had not been there a day before a wealthy Spanish grandee, married to a titled Roman lady, brought us to his palace to stay. He had had letters from the King and from nobles in Spain, and was determined that Master should lodge with him.

He was Don Rodrigo de Foncerrada, elderly, kindly and stout. He and his lady had had a large family of daughters, but all were married and living in their own homes, and he had many rooms in his palace. There we were established, and Don Rodrigo accorded Master every honor, giving him a suite of several rooms, one of which he cleared of all unnecessary furniture and used as a studio. I slept on a pallet in the same room, as I had always done on journeys, so as to be able to look after him at all times.

There is no doubt that both Don Rodrigo and his lady were intimates of the Pope and of his Vatican officials, for it was only a matter of days before a special emissary arrived with gifts and greetings and Master was invited to a special audience with Pope Innocent X.

I remember that Master prepared for this with great care. He fasted and went to confession and Communion; he bathed and had me wash his hair. He dressed as always, in black, good Spanish custom. Don Rodrigo, too, wore only black, or a very dark green, but his lady, old and wrinkled as she was, and lacking some teeth, painted her hair a metallic gold and wore dresses of scarlet, violet, and apricot.

Master set off for the Vatican alone, but he had not gone twenty steps before he returned for me.

"Juanico, come walk with me. You will have to wait somewhere while the Pope receives me, but you have been at my side on this whole Italian journey and I would like to know that you are not far away when I kiss the ring of His Holiness."

So we walked together through those streets where so many countless generations of feet had trod, since long before the days of Our Lord. . . . We passed tall columns the Romans had brought home from their wars of conquest and had set up proudly in their own squares, to remind the citizens of how far Roman arms had carried power. And there were many churches, built at different periods in time, some unfinished. We came to the Tiber, rushing green and violently swollen from spring freshets between its deep-carved banks, and we walked along the river's edge for some way, leaving Castel Sant'Angelo on our right.

In less than an hour's time, for Rome is not a far-flung city, we came to that impressive semi-circle which stretches out from St. Peter's like two encircling arms. I went with Master as far as I could before the guards turned me back, and then I returned to St. Peter's, to pray.

I knelt a long time, for I had much to offer up to God, and I placed before Him countless thoughts, so that He might winnow them like a thresher, leaving me the wheat and blowing away the chaff with the breath of His mercy. When I rose my knees were stiff and I felt tired and old, though I had not then completed forty years. But I was strengthened in good resolutions and at peace, and so I gave myself the pleasure of strolling from altar to altar in that enormous, impressive church. I paused a long time before the sculptured Virgin, sorrowing with her dead Son in her arms; it was a Pietà of Michelangelo, so moving and tender that it brought tears springing to the eyes.

Master had told me that after his audience he would seek me in the church, and there he found me, in front of the Pietà. He did not say a word, nor did I, but we stood there, looking and marveling for a long time. Then Master touched me lightly, in signal that we would leave, and we went out into the brilliant morning sunshine.

"Let us take some refreshment," he said, and we sat at a small outdoor table. A serving maid brought us wine and olives and slices of strongly flavored sausage.

"I am asked to paint a portrait of His Holiness," Master announced abruptly, removing an olive pit from his mouth.

"Oh, Master! Oh, God be praised! Now they will recognize you for what you are all over Italy! All over the whole world!"

"I think His Majesty, our King, suggested it. It was arranged from abroad. But I could see that some of the Vatican court nobles are less than enthusiastic. They do not like foreigners in general and Spaniards in particular. I must do a superb portrait, Juanico."

"You will."

"I wish I were as certain of it as you are."

He called for a basket of cherries and began to eat them, offering me some, but I found them too sour. They were the first cherries of spring, rather pale in color.

"I feel uneasy about this portrait. I must do some practice studies first. I arranged for the first sitting a month from now." He began to flex his hand and stare unhappily at his fingers.

"Paint me, Master! Paint a portrait of me!"

He had often made sketches of me and set the apprentices to painting me, but now I saw him studying me with a new look, a cool detached, intent look. I saw him mentally drawing my round cheek, my heavy nose and lips, the line of my mustache and beard, my eyes.

"Come," he said, pushing away his wine and fruit. "Come, we will buy a canvas. Yes, I will paint you, Juanico. As you are, loyal and resourceful and good. And also proud and dignified. God guide my hand."

Twelve

In which my portrait is painted

THERE was a large window to the north in the room we were using as a studio, through which poured a clear shadowless light all day.

Master said I was to wear my everyday clothes, only he gave me a large white collar with deep points, lace-edged (one of his own), to set off the somber darkness of my dress and my dusky complexion.

He placed me before him, told me to look directly at him, and to clasp my cloak so that it should fall over my left shoulder.

It was an easy pose. I had posed for pupils in his studio at home, when I would almost topple over with weariness before I was given the signal to break pose, but this was nothing. I simply stood. The expression was what was harder to remember. Master wanted me to look at him as if he were a stranger, a passerby, a mere person. He wanted, he said, that look of dignity, with a hint of caution and reserve.

We worked steadily every day, as long as there was light, and soon I got used to taking the same pose, corrected by a movement of Master's hand to right or left, and to assuming the same emotion inside me which gave Master the expression he wanted.

On the second day he began laying on the color. As was his custom, he dropped a drape over his work each day, and he never allowed the model to see what he was doing. At the end of the fourth day, he called me to look.

There I stood, looking at myself, as if in a mirror. All apart from the likeness, which was startling (Master had no peer at that), the composition was harmonious and impressive in typical Spanish fashion, and yet there was an unusual glow of golden light around my head and on my skin, and an inner content which I can scarcely describe. It was as if Master had painted what you see on the outside, and also, just as clearly, what was there in the inside . . . the thoughts inside my head.

"Master, not because it is your Juanico, but I think it is the best you have ever painted! I see myself, and I know what I am thinking!"

Master gave me his brushes.

"I am content," he said, and that was all. I took his brushes away to wash them, and as I prepared the soapy water and washed the color out of them I began to work out some details of a bold idea I had had a few days before.

I knew, I had gathered from gossip overheard and from remarks Master had made, that there were intrigues at the court of the Vatican, as elsewhere in Europe and, no doubt, all over the world. People are the same everywhere, and the Italians had long considered that they were the only true artists in Europe. It did not sit well with them that a Spaniard had been chosen to paint the portrait of His Holiness. It was significant to me, and could not have escaped Master, that not one Roman noble had come forward to ask Master for a portrait. I intended to shame them into that, and soon.

As soon as my portrait was dry enough to carry, I put my plan into action. I had armed myself with the names of about ten of the great patrons of painting in Rome. Then I waited for a morning when Master was busy with personal errands, and gave me some time to myself. It came soon enough, and I set out. I took the painting and covered it carefully to protect it from dust and against any accident in the street, and I went to the home of the Duke of Ponti. A rather insolent house servant in livery came to ask me my business at the door, and I told him that I must speak to the Duke; I had a message from Don Diego Rodríguez de Silva y Velázquez, who was engaged to paint a portrait of His Holiness. I thought that would bring him, and it did. The doors were shortly opened to me, and I was ushered into the presence of the Duke himself. He was lolling in a reclining chair, enveloped to the chin in a white sheet, whilst his barber cut and curled his hair.

I stood in the doorway until the Duke shouted, "Come in, come in! What is this message, hey?"

I let him push the barber aside, sit up and look at me in anger. Then I said, "I understand that you are interested in portraiture, and I thought you might like to look at this one, your honor."

I flung back the cover and set up the portrait by my side.

I had taken care to dress in the same clothes and also to wear the white collar, and I could hear the Duke gasp.

"By Bacchus!" he shouted. "*That* is a portrait!"

"It is a work dashed off by my Master in the last few days, merely to relax," I told him. "He is the greatest portraitist in Europe."

The Duke stood up, clucked unhappily, and showed every evidence of being mightily annoyed.

"I will agree," he said at last, without pleasure. "He is. Fellow, what is your name?"

"Juan de Pareja."

"I would like you to take this portrait and show it to a friend of mine. Will you do it?" Suddenly he threw back his head and laughed. "No, wait! I would like to make a wager with him first, for I have need of fifty ducats. No. Come here tomorrow at this same hour, with the portrait."

"I am not interested in your honor's wagers," I answered, with dignity, "but in securing commissions and recognition for my Master."

The Duke stared at me, then laughed again, and shrugged his shoulders.

"So be it. You will get commissions enough, I promise you. But I can see that stiff-necked Spanish pride in the servant as well as the Master; you are all alike. So I will be the first to offer Messer Velázquez a commission. I will call on him this very afternoon to order a painting of my wife. Now, will you come in the morning, as I asked?"

"I will come."

I went back to where we were living then, and I was well pleased.

That very afternoon the Duke of Ponti arrived resplendent in violet silk brocade figured with gold threads and shoes with golden buckles. He swept from his head a wide-brimmed velvet hat with a green plume, and bowed low. Master, in his severe black, looking slight and pale, received him with grave courtesy, and after they had taken wine, Master agreed to paint a portrait of the Duchess. The Duke said nothing about me and my portrait, nor did I.

But next morning, I carried out my promise. There was a stout Italian nobleman with him, a pale-eyed man who had a repulsive habit of taking his lower lip between his fingers, pulling it out, and then letting it snap back with a flopping sound.

Evidently the wager had been made, for a portrait of the stout person stood near and I had a quick glance at it. It had been done in a mannered way, the features softened and prettified, and the colors were all in the pale spectrum. I had an idea, then, of what I was there for, so I stood and waited until the Duke asked me to unwrap my portrait. I am not inexperienced about the best light in which to display a painting, and I had chosen my place. I took my position and set beside me that other self which was my portrait. The stout man stared, pulled at his lip, and then tossed a little bag of ducats to his friend. The Duke of Ponti took out a ducat and threw it toward me, but

Master always kept me well and gave me money when I needed it, so I let it fall to the floor and did not stoop to pick it up.

"Come, Juan, take the ducat as a gift."

"I will be glad to accept it as a gift," I told him, "when it is so given."

I will say for the honor of the Duke of Ponti that he came, picked up the ducat and offered it to me, with a bow.

As I left I heard the man who had lost the wager asking for Master's address, and I knew another commission was on its way.

In this way, after I had called on seven or eight more of the city's rich noblemen, Master received commissions enough to keep him busy all year. Best of all, I knew that now these people would become his defenders and his champions before the others who wished to exclude the Spanish master from the highest circles of Rome. To their credit, I must say that those Italians, once convinced, were most generous, gallant, and flattering, and Master himself was almost repulsed by so much adulation. He was always one to demand honor due as a man and as an artist, but now they made him into an idol and it was not to his taste.

However, he was soon immersed in the work of painting the portrait of His Holiness and seemed to forget everything else, though he carried out all his commissions meticulously and perfectly on days when he had no sittings with the Pope. Forgotten entirely was his distress and worry about his painting hand. That hand was now more skillful than ever.

When at last he brought home the first study paintings of His Holiness, before he began on the final large canvas which would be the portrait, I studied them with care. The heads showed the Pope to be a man of strength and power; it was a cruel, even a wicked, face, I thought. But I withheld any judgment; no doubt the Pope, who had to rule many rebellious powerful persons and groups, had need of more than heavenly perceptions.

When Master began his final work in earnest, he took me along as he always did, to being colors, change brushes, and perform all those other duties which were mine when he was working intensely. I watched the work grow, and I could see, even in the beginning, that it was going to be the greatest portrait he had ever done because the magnificent studies of our King, fine though they were, could only show the reserve, the sadness, and the nobility of His Majesty, whereas the Pope was a man in whose eyes thousands of subtle thoughts flickered constantly.

As the work grew I became a little anxious for Master, as I saw the face of the pontiff emerging a sharp, ambitious, a difficult man. Could such things be? Perhaps. I was given a short lesson in this regard by Master himself.

We walked back from the Vatican one day, after the Pope had posed, and Master seemed in a mellow mood. He was whistling softly to himself, and I took courage to ask him a question.

"Master, may not His Holiness be offended when he sees how you have painted him?"

"Offended because I have shown him as he is? Not a handsome face, not even a merciful one. Is that what you mean, Juanico?"

"Yes."

"Well, he will see himself, and he is used to himself, to what he sees reflected in the mirror. I rather think he is man enough to be pleased that I have seen him as tough and strong; he would not relish weakness in anyone, least of all in his own portrait. But we are all a bit fond of our own faces, Juanico, no matter how they seem to others. Even I."

At all events, Master's portrait of the Pope was a resounding success. Almost immediately he had to paint the Pope's nephew, Cardinal Pamphili, a strikingly elegant man, and before we left Rome he had done many more.

It was getting on for Christmas when Master called a halt, finished up all his pending business, and made arrangements for us to start home again.

Our journey was not pleasant, but it was not too bad. We had no storms, and even the overland stretches were not too bitterly cold. We were happy indeed to see the faces of our own once again. Doña Paquita and her little daughter, and Don Juan Bautista del Mazo stood by the side of Mistress to welcome us back, and in the happy cries and tearful embraces, not even I was left out, but everyone made me feel that I too had been missed, and now that we were back, Master and I, life would take on color and savor once more.

Before a week had gone by Master and I had walked through the familiar streets to the studio in the palace again, and had set out all Master's canvases once more. It had been a rule for a long time now that all Master's work should be stacked about, face against the walls, so that the King, whenever he wished to, could walk in, turn one around, and sit and gaze at it as long as he wished. He had ordered Master never to stop working or bow or await his pleasure, when he was painting. Now we prepared for those casual visits of Majesty, which took place so often.

Master was called to the throne room for a long formal report of his journey and a display of all the art treasures he had collected. Afterward there was to be a great state banquet to welcome him back.

For me, the homecoming was happy, but also deeply disturbing, for Mistress had acquired a new slave while I was in Italy. A female. Her name was Lolis, and she was in charge of the kitchen, of buying stores, and of looking after Mistress, who was much troubled with a cough, night fevers and weakness, and could not attend to her household any more. Lolis was a quiet woman of my race; she went softly about her duties. She never began any conversations with me, but as we ate together often in the kitchen I began to ask her questions, to learn something of what her life had been. Her voice, when she answered, enchanted me; it was low and throaty, with a softness like velvet, and yet it carried amazingly. She was not beautiful as Miri had been, in her delicate, elongated, slender way. Lolis was fullbodied, strong-boned. But she carried herself well, and she had grace and power. Nor did she give Miri's impression of being gentle and weak. Lolis was quiet and silent, but she was strong and proud and hot-tempered. She learned to control her temper when she must, but I often saw her explode in fury against some inanimate object, and then her dark eyes sparkled with amber lights and her dusky skin paled.

"I belonged to the Duchess of Mancera; I nursed her through her last illness," Lolis told me. "That lady was a friend of your Mistress. And when the Duke began rearranging his household for his second marriage, he thought me too young and too . . . shall I say, troublesome . . . for his young second wife. He did not wish to remind her in any way of the first Duchess. Vain old pig, he is." But she laughed forgivingly. "He recommended me to Mistress, and she bought me. Now I shall nurse her till she dies. And then. . . ."

"What do you mean?" I cried out, alarmed. "Is Mistress really seriously ill?"

Lolis looked at me pityingly. Then she shrugged. "She doesn't yet know it. But Death has his eye on her."

"Oh," I cried, feeling tears stinging my eyelids. "What will Master do when she is gone?"

"What they all do," she said, cynically. "Marry again as fast as he can."

"Master is different," I told her.

She stood and looked at me sadly.

"I can see that you love these white people," she said then. "I do not."

"They have been good to me."

She started to speak, and I saw her pale as she did when she was angry, but then she checked herself.

"I would not have you bitter and rebellious, as I am," she said then, gently. "It is too hard, hiding it, and waiting. Waiting, always. You are a good man. Be happy."

"Do you know much of illness . . . and death?" I asked then, still thinking of Mistress.

"Enough. My mother taught me many things. She taught me to tell the future, too," she cried merrily, in one of her sudden changes of mood. "Come, let me see your hand!"

She put out her hand, broad-palmed, long-fingered, on the table between us. It was very clean and soft; I could scarcely bring myself to lay my big paint-stained hand upon it.

"Don't then!" she cried, pettishly, and slapped at me. But she was not angry. "Even without seeing your palm, I can tell you your future."

Another day she coaxed, "Let me see your hand, Juan. Do."

I laid it, palm upward, on a table, for her to see. She studied it a long time, a frown wrinkling the soft skin between her eyebrows.

"You will confer a title on someone after he is dead," she told me, in a wondering voice, "and you too, will have honors heaped upon you after you are laid in earth."

"Uuuug." I shivered. "I do not like your fortune telling."

She stared at me in puzzlement.

"It is so strange," she murmured. "Your future is soft and shadowy, but when you are dead it will be golden."

Lolis often saw the future, she told me, as if it had been rolled down before her eyes like a painted curtain, and upon it she read all that was to come to pass.

One day she came to seek me in the studio, where I was stretching canvas, Master having been bidden to wait upon the King in his apartments.

"It has happened again," she said, looking excited and pleased.

"But what?"

"The curtain came down before me, and I saw."

"Something good? You seem happy."

She laughed at me, letting her dark eyes rest on me, and I saw mischief and fun . . . and something else . . . in her expression.

"Yes. Something good," she said.

She seemed gayer in the days that followed, less subject to her angers and tempers. And besides, as Mistress grew weaker, Lolis seemed to grow more tender with her. She began really to love her, I think.

As for me, love had come and bloomed in my heart. Lolis was not gentle and sweet like my mother, nor pitifully delicate and lovely like Miri. She was a person with her own character and with great variety in her makeup. She was constantly interesting to me, and I looked forward to hearing her soft step, to listening to her wonderful deep laughter, to those occasions when she touched me or even slapped at me as she went about her work.

Master had told me in Italy, had given me his solemn promise, that he would give me whatever I asked for when I had made his hand well.

I knew that it was not I, but God, who had cured him. Nevertheless, I intended now to ask Master for something. I would ask him to give me Lolis for my wife.

But first I must keep my promise to Our Lady, and I had thought of a way to do it.

Thirteen

In which I am made free

THE King was in the habit of coming often, at odd hours, to pass a short while in the studio.

"You have only to see me as your sovereign when I speak," he told Master. "I wish to be able to slip in and out, quietly, without any formality, to sit and enjoy a painting of my choosing, and feel at peace." He had given me orders that I was not to "see" him either unless he spoke, whenever he came unaccompanied. "I wish to spend a little time in complete invisibility," he told us, smiling.

So cakes and wine were always waiting for him in the studio, and one of his own easy chairs. His accustomed hour to drop in was late afternoon, before he had to dress for some court function.

Long ago I had heard some of the courtiers in Rubens' train say that the Spanish court was the stiffest and most boring in Europe. I am sure His Majesty found it so, but did not know what to do about it.

So he escaped, and sat sipping his wine, and gazing at some picture of Master's, which he had turned round from where they were stacked, and set up, at some distance from his chair.

I had secretly painted a large canvas, for Master was frequently in attendance on Mistress in her bedroom, where she rested many hours, and to which she called him to chat with her. She often felt lonely and needed him near.

My subject was the King's favorite hounds. All were dead, and they had not been contemporaries, but they had been favorites of his, and I knew that he would recognize them.

The three hounds (one of them was Corso) lay in a forest glade; a shaft of golden light came through the branches of the trees and lay warmly on them. One dog was turned toward me, tongue drooping from his mouth, the black doggy lips turned up in a smile; one looked away into the distance with pricked ears; and one dozed, nose on paws. I had taken their likenesses carefully from many paintings of Master, and I had worked out the setting with all the art of which I was capable.

Having received Communion and commended myself to Our Lady, I took that canvas and put it amongst those of Master turned against the wall, to await the King's pleasure. Then, trembling and already frightened, I awaited the hour when I would have to confess.

Several days went by. His Majesty was indisposed and remained in his apartments.

Master was painting another mirror arrangement, fussily moving his mirrors about, checking lights and reflections; he paid no attention to me and did not notice that I was nervous.

Then my hour struck.

It was late in the afternoon. Master was not painting, but sitting at his desk making out some accounts and writing to order special pigments from Flanders. The door of the studio opened quietly and His Majesty stepped in, looking around in his uncertain, apologetic way. He was dressed for some court ceremony: black velvet shoes and long black silk stockings, black velvet trousers, but instead of a doublet he wore only a white shirt of thin cotton, and a dressing gown of dark silk brocade. I supposed that after contemplating a picture he meant to return to his rooms, put on his doublet, call the barber to shave him and curl his hair and mustache, and then attach his big white starched ruff at the last moment.

He pulled out his chair, sat, and stretched his long legs with a deep sigh. He smiled amiably at Master, who smiled back warmly, affectionately, and then went on with his accounts.

After a short time the King rose and went toward the wall. He stood hesitating a moment, and then turned a canvas toward him. It was mine. In the late light, the faithful hounds shone out from the dark background, sunlight on their glistening hides, light in their big, loving, dark eyes. His Majesty stood transfixed; he had never seen that canvas before. I could watch his always-slow mind adjusting to the fact that this was a portrait of his own favorite hounds.

I threw myself on my knees before him.

"I beg mercy, Sire," I pleaded. "The painting is mine. I have been working secretly all these years, with bits of canvas and color, copying the works of Master, to learn from them, and trying some original subjects by myself. I know very well that this is against the law. Master has never even suspected and has had nothing to do with my treachery. I am willing to endure whatever punishment you mete out to me."

I remained on my knees, begging the Virgin to remember my promise, praying and asking her forgiveness and her help. Opening my eyes, I saw the feet of His Majesty moving nervously about. Evidently he did not know what to reply. Then he cleared his throat and took a deep breath. The feet in the velvet shoes remained quiet.

"What . . . what shall we do . . . with this . . . this . . . disobedient slave?" I heard his voice lisping and stuttering, as he turned toward Master.

Still on my knees, I saw Master's neat small feet, in their shoes of Cordovan leather, approach and place themselves in front of my picture. He studied it some time in silence, and the King waited.

Then Master spoke. "Have I your Majesty's leave to write an urgent letter before I answer?"

"You have it."

Master returned to his desk and I heard his quill scratching against the paper. His Majesty returned to his chair and threw himself into it. I remained where I was, praying with all my might.

Master rose, and his feet moved toward me.

"Get up, Juan," he said. He put a hand under my elbow and helped me to my feet. He was looking at me with the gentle affection he had always shown me.

He took my hand and put a letter into it. I have worn that letter sewed into a silk envelope and pinned inside my shirt ever since. The letter said:

To Whom It May Concern

I have this day given freedom to my slave Juan de Pareja, who shall have all the rights and honors of a free man, and further, I hereby name him my Assistant, with the duties and salary thereto pertaining.

DIEGO RODRÍGUEZ DE SILVA Y VELÁZQUEZ

Master took the letter gently from my hand, after I had read it, and took it to the King who, reading, smiled radiantly. It was the first time in all those years that I had seen His Majesty smile. His teeth were small and uneven, but that smile seemed to me as beautiful as any I had ever seen.

The letter was given back to me, and I stood there, tears of joy streaming from my eyes.

"You were saying, Sire, something about a slave?" inquired Master softly. "I have no slave."

I seized his hand, to carry it to my lips.

"No, no," cried Master, snatching his hand back. "You owe me no gratitude, my good friend. The contrary. I am ashamed that in my selfish preoccupations I did not long ago give you what you have earned so well and what I know you will grace with your many virtues. You are to be my assistant if you wish, as you are my friend always."

"I am pleased," said His Majesty, and rose to his feet. At the door, before he left, he turned and said again, "I am pleased."

We waited, Master and I, side by side, bowing, as the King sailed down the corridor, his dressing gown billowing out behind him.

"Let us pack up our things, Juan (he never again called me Juanico), and go home. Mistress is fretful when I am not more often at her side. And I am tired."

"As your assistant, Master . . ."

"Now do not call me Master any more. Call me Diego."

"I cannot. You are still Master. My Master, as you were Master to the apprentices, and to other painters. Master means teacher, does it not?"

"Yes."

"I was never ashamed to call you my Master, and I am not ashamed now. I shall always give you the respect of that title."

"As you wish."

We were walking through the streets of Madrid toward our home. I took each step with a new spring in my knees, a new joy in my heart, for I walked as a free man, beside my Teacher.

"But, Master," I said, as we crossed the Plaza Mayor, "you were in error when you said that you had no slave. There is Lolis."

"Lolis belongs to my wife," he told me.

I determined to make this a day radiant in my memory in every way.

"Master, when we were in Italy, you told me that I could ask anything of this hand" (and I took his right hand lightly in my own) "and you would give it me. Now I know what to ask for."

He stopped in the square where the last rays of the sun struck level against us. "You want Lolis," he said, smiling.

"I wish to marry her. If she will have me."

"I will speak to my wife about it. I see no reason why you should not marry if you both wish it," he answered, and we continued to stroll in silence.

Inside our house—that house where I had lived so many years in peace of mind and spirit, even though I had not been free—everything now seemed new to me. The corridors, so much a part of my daily existence, the dark heavy carved furniture, the life-sized crucifix with its small glow and flicker of light always in a glass bowl at the feet of the Christ, the dark red velvet curtains now drawn against the declining day to keep out the humors and evils of night—all were dear and known to me, but somehow fresh and new.

We had no sooner entered than Lolis came running toward us, finger to lip.

"The Mistress has been in much pain today," she whispered, "and I have just now been able to get her to sleep."

"I will not go up then," answered Master. "Bring us some wine, please, Lolis, and some walnuts."

We went into the dining room. Very often Paquita came, with her little daughter, but today the house was quiet and still. We ate our nuts and drank wine together. I could see that Master was worried, and I knew why. Mistress was more and more often ill and weak, and sometimes she lay and cried.

When I went into the kitchen later Lolis came and laid her head on my shoulder. She was not weeping—I have always been quick to tears, but I have never seen one glittering on her lashes—but she sighed deeply.

"My poor lady," she grieved. "I have come to be fond of her, Juan. And soon we will have to give her some opium to stop the awful paroxysms of coughing. The King could get it for Master. It will be a sad time now, Juan, until God calls her."

Actually, as sometimes happens, Mistress rallied and seemed much better a few days later. She got up and was dressed and began to eat some of the dainties Lolis had prepared for her. On the second evening she came to the supper table and smiled and seemed very happy, sitting at Master's side. She ate quite a bit of supper and did not cough once.

Master looked up at me suddenly and I could read his intention in his eyes. Turning to her, he said, "*Mi vida*, I have given our good friend Juan his freedom and he is now my honored assistant. He will take many duties off my shoulders and I will rest more and be more often with you. I know you have been lonely with our daughter married and gone from the house."

"Ah yes!" cried Mistress, her thin face lighting up. "That is why I have been ailing. I have been lonely."

"And Juan wishes to marry. He has given his heart to you, Lolis. What do you say?"

Mistress clasped her hands. "Lolis!" she cried. "What is your answer?"

I remember that Lolis was wearing a dress of pale almond green, and she had bound back her hair with a rose-colored scarf.

"I can answer as I wish?" asked Lolis.

"Of course."

"My answer is No."

I felt as if my heart had been pierced with a dagger. Lolis saw the hurt in my face.

"It is not that I do not like him," she said, in her deep soft voice. "He is a good kind man, but I do not wish to bear any children into slavery."

Master's quiet voice was heard. "You are right, Lolis. Juan is now a free man. And I am sure my wife would like to give you your freedom, as a wedding gift. Isn't it so, my love?"

Mistress took her cue and answered at once, for she was always eager to please Master in every way she knew, and now that she was ill, more than ever, it seemed.

"It is so indeed. If you will hand me the paper and pen and inkpot, I will write the letter of manumission now."

Mistress wrote the letter and put it into Lolis' hand.

"My dear Lolis," she said, "you are as free now, as you have always been in your spirit, I think. But I would ask a favor of you. Please stay on as my nurse. Do not leave me . . . just yet."

Lolis put the letter in her bosom, and she looked with tenderness at Mistress.

"I am glad to be free," she said. "More than you can know. I never dreamed that it would come to pass so soon, though I had seen in the future that it would be so, one day. Just as I have seen that I would marry Juan. Yes, I shall stay with you, Mistress, as long as you want me. And I thank you."

Quietly she gathered up some dishes and left the room softly.

Master gave me permission with his eyes, and I followed Lolis out into the kitchen. She was in a corner, on her knees, praying.

"I was thanking God," she told me. "I have prayed for this every day of my life."

"And you will marry me, Lolis?"

"Yes. But you could have found a better woman, Juan. I am proud and haughty and sometimes I have a sharp tongue."

"It is you I want, just as you are."

She came into my arms then, and let me caress her hair, her cheek and her forehead.

"I have resented being a slave," she said. "I could not feel grateful in my heart, for deep inside me I resented being bound. I know that God made us all free and that no man should own another. I hated serving people because I was a slave and had to do their will. Only here in this house I had some peace because you are all kind and Mistress is sweet and affectionate. I will do my best to make her last days comfortable. But I am not like you, Juan, grateful and loving. I *hated* being owned! It was all I could do, some days, to keep the hot words inside my mouth and the resentment out of my voice."

"Never mind. Everything is different now. And if we have children, they will be born free."

"Yes. But many of our race are not, Juan. My heart aches for them."

"Some day," I assured her, "some day, I know that all men will be free."

"It will take a long time, and much bloodshed, before that day comes," said Lolis, somberly.

Fourteen

In which I say a sad good-by

LOLIS and I were married in the church near our house, where, since Murillo had encouraged me, I had confessed and received Communion regularly. Paquita, who was expecting another child, and her husband stood up with us, and dear Master was there at my side. Mistress had had several bad days and was very weak, but she gave us her blessing before we went to the church.

My heart was swollen with happiness as I clasped the hand of my dear Lolis and heard the words which made us man and wife, from that day forward, forever. So soon I was to thank God most fervently that he had given me my tender companion before all our sorrow came upon us, for without her I do not think I could have stood it. That was a terrible year for us.

Mistress had given Lolis a length of blue silk from which she had made her wedding gown. Master gave us chairs and rugs and two rooms in his house, which were to be our apartments, and even the King sent us a gift: a velvet bag with thirty ducats in it.

Then heaven showered down on us very hard trials. Paquita did not survive the birth of her child, despite all Dr. Méndez's skill, and the infant was stillborn. They were buried together, the little innocent, and our merry, affectionate Paquita. At first we did not dare to tell Mistress, and our misgivings were based on truth, because when at last she had to know, she went into her final decline.

Dr. Méndez arranged for her to have opium at the last, and she was allowed to sleep away her days and nights, racked by the coughing, but not feeling it in her drugged dreams.

Not two months after we had laid Paquita and her baby in the earth, we took Mistress to lie by her side.

Master did not shed one tear, but turned silent and cold. He did not speak, nor answer any questions, and many days he would not eat anything but a little fruit. He became very thin and pale and paid no attention to anything that happened around him. I think, if I had not been at his side, he would not have washed or changed his clothes. He was not himself. His spirit was far away, in some country where I could not follow.

In those days His Majesty proved what a true friend he was to Master. Not one day went by that he did not come, and simply sit, quiet and comforting in his big silent presence, in the same room where Master was.

As the winter wore away and spring came on, Master began to draw again, for the reason, I believe, that he had lived with a charcoal stick or a brush in his hand for so long that he automatically took them up again, even when his heart was breaking. He worked unceasingly then, but mostly he tore up or destroyed anything he drew or painted. I was sometimes able to save and preserve something; those are my treasures, today.

Then one day the King came to the studio, preceded by pages. He was dressed in blue, and a proclamation was read, as everyone stood at attention.

The court crier announced that the King's sister, the Infanta Maria Teresa, was to marry King Louis XIV of France. The bridegroom would not appear, but was to be married by proxy. Nevertheless, the ceremonies were to be of the most brilliant possible, and Don Diego Rodríguez de Silva y Velázquez, Court Painter, was put in charge of the design and decoration of the pavilion where the ceremony was to take place.

After the King had gone, with his criers, Master sat down and began to sketch at once. I knew, as he did, that this would be a task calling into play all his qualities. He would have to consult with the architects, the builders, the caterers, the tailors and dressmakers. A royal wedding is always a brilliant affair, but this was to be tremendously important as well, since Louis XIV was the most powerful monarch in Europe, and even though he would not attend, but would be represented by a proxy, there would be plenty of French courtiers present to report to him. I could see that the challenge to Master might be of enormous effect upon his health as well; he was always one to take his duties to heart, and he wished to make the King very proud of him. The whole matter took possession of his mind and drew it away from sadness and pining. Before a month had gone by, he was almost himself again.

We journeyed together to investigate the site which the King had chosen for the pavilion. It was a beautiful island in the middle of the River Bidassoa, but it was marshy and somewhat low. At night a miasma covered those green meadows, and early in the morning swarms of mosquitoes rose from them in clouds. Later they were dispersed by the heat of the sun.

There was no doubt that a pavilion there would be enchantingly beautiful, and could do no harm, in that it was to be used only that one day. However, we had to work out there day after day, calculating, studying, deciding, sketching, and it was an unhealthy place.

Despite my fears, however, Master remained well, and so did I, though many of the workmen who began the building went down with fever, and some of them died. Not too much importance was attached to this, as we always had a certain number of deaths in summer from fever.

Whenever I could, I took from Master's shoulders some of the tiresome tasks of inspection, while he painted and perfected his designs in the studio. Toward the end he was often at the pavilion, making certain that all his instructions were being carried out. When all was ready, it was rich and dignified, in the finest Spanish tradition, embodying in itself all the splendor and power of the Spanish royal house.

Master had designed a great rectangular courtyard, covered with stone and with finely fitted planks of dark wood, over which the most glowing of carpets had been laid, in tones of dark and of pale leaf green. Arches lifted slender arms over the whole pavilion, but they were not closed in by a roof. We were certain rain would not fall, and Master had arranged for light lattices to be laid between the arches, and around and between them grew vines, blossoming with fragrant small white flowers. Standing below, and looking up through the flowers and leaves, one had a sensation of coolness and purity beyond compare.

The altar was white and gold, except for the large crucifix. Master had painted the canvases with which it was adorned. There were two tall angels, robed in white, pictures of St. Joseph and of Santiago, and above the altar a most beautiful painting of Our Lady. All the paintings had been done rather differently from Master's custom, for the backgrounds were not in his favorite, deep-shadowed style, but delicately shot with silvery light.

All along the route of the wedding procession, he placed paintings of tall white urns of flowers, alternating these with urns of flowers themselves, and behind each was a mirror. The effect was that of being inside a great bower of blooms, but Master's paintings and mirrors saved the atmosphere from becoming too cloyingly sweet with the flowers' fragrance. He did not want the Infanta or any of her ladies to be overcome, and faint, on that momentous occasion.

The wedding party were to be dressed in various shades of green, all except the Princess and the King. She wore white, and from the golden hair of the Princess, bound to her head by a chaplet of white flowers, fell a long veil of white gauze. His Majesty was clothed in cloth of silver, with embroideries and in- sets of pale green.

That wedding was indeed the most beautiful ceremony I have ever seen, and I am sure none of the nobles who attended had ever dreamed of anything so fair, in such perfect taste, repre- senting so exquisitely the hope, the purity, and youth of a young bride.

Master and I returned to Madrid, where he was, of course, in- vited to all the routs, dances, and banquets which were to fol- low, celebrating the wedding. But when the King announced a great hunt and feast before the departure of the bride for France, Master excused himself, saying that he was weary and his head ached.

I did not worry at first, for Master did not like hunts and never rode if he could help it, and besides, he had been subject on occasions to bad headaches, and I knew how to take care of him. He returned to our house in the city, lay down, and I dark- ened his room and put cool cloths on his brow. The day was very hot and sticky, but I soon realized that he was feverish. He tore open the front of his light lawn shirt and lay panting, and when I raised the shades slightly I saw that this was not one of his migraines, when he became pale and cold, but a fever. His cheeks were darkly flushed, and his eyes were shining like porcelain. His brow felt very hot to my hand.

Lolis helped me nurse him. We did everything we knew, and to my store of knowledge about diseases Lolis added hers. Be- sides, of course, we called in Dr. Méndez, who had us keep Mas- ter hot under blankets, sweating as much as possible. Lolis and I implored Master to take the hot broths she prepared, and teas heavily sweetened with honey. He was obedient, but the fever was persistent, and despite all our efforts it came back every night toward sundown, to shake and consume him. It usually broke with a sweat in the mornings, and then I could sponge him and make him comfortable on fresh cool sheets, and he would drowse a while. But then, toward late afternoon, Master would waken and lie waiting, anxious and weak, and the fevers would start up their flames again. I remembered that in just this dumb, helpless way, he had set himself to endure the mis- eries of seasickness on our voyages.

Despite everything, all our nursing and prayers, and all Dr. Méndez's nostrums, the fever lasted for twenty-one days, and at the end of it Master was a skeleton. He had never been a heavy

man and had always been a light, delicate eater. He had no re-
serves of strength. The King came every day, though he could
not speak, for emotion, and only sat and stared at Master with
his pale, sad eyes.

Then came a day when Master awaited the fever, and it held
off and held off. The night came, and passed. Master slept
deeply, and he was cool and quiet. Lolis and I fell into each
other's arms, laughing and weeping. The fever was broken. Master would get well.

The convalescence was slow, of course. Little by little Master
must be induced to eat again, a bit more every day, to regain his
strength. Then we let him sit up, bolstered about with cushions.
At last the doctor said he could get up and walk about in his room.

It was a Tuesday. The day dawned fair and clear, and there
were patterns of sunlight on the polished wood of the studio
floor. I held a mirror, so that Master could sit up and shave himself. He slipped on a long Arabic robe that came down to his
heels, and soft leather slippers, swung his legs round, and set
them on the floor, for the first time in weeks.

"I must lean on you, Juan, I think, if you please. I am still
rather weak."

He stood up and I took his weight (so much less now, though
it was never much) on my shoulder. We walked slowly through
the hall and into the studio. Master sighed with joy to be there,
with his easels and his paintings in view. It was coming back to
life. He sat and rested a time. Then he rose again, and we
started toward his favorite easel, where a piece of stretched canvas awaited him.

Half-way there, gently disengaging himself, he started forward
alone. But he did not reach the easel. Almost there he tottered,
put out his hand to grasp something, and fell prone. I was there
as soon as he was, cursing myself for having let him try to walk
alone. As I raised him I saw that I could do nothing. He was
gone. Sorrow and the illness had weakened his heart, and at the
first effort it had fluttered to a stop.

I sat there on the floor, cradling him in my arms, remembering all our years together. I, who had always had facile tears,
could not shed one. I felt the dark wings of the angel of death
enfolding my Master, my Teacher, and it seemed that they must
enfold me too, with him.

It was Lolis who took care of everything while I stood about
helpless and useless. She called Dr. Méndez, who came and
made the formal pronouncements. She advised the King, who

came and kept vigil all night at Master's bier. I stood stony-faced and dry-eyed, but His Majesty wept the night through.

Master was given a quiet funeral and laid to rest by the side of Mistress and near Paquita, who had gone on such a short time before. He had left no will, but the King knew his wishes, and they were carried out. I was overwhelmed with gifts—all his clothes, his easel and a goodly sum of money. All his household effects were left to Paquita's husband, and the house, where we had all lived so long and so many happy years, was for Paquita's eldest child, the little granddaughter Master had loved so much and painted so often.

Lolis and I talked over our future when I was able to pull myself together and face the fact that there were still years ahead, years when I must work and take care of my wife and carry out whatever tasks God still had awaiting me.

"I think," I told her, "that I would like to return to Seville. Madrid is too sad for me now."

"I, too, would like to live in the south, nearer Africa," she told me, and so we began to pack our boxes and make our farewell calls.

I begged an audience with His Majesty, to take leave of him.

He was dressed in black and received me like a man in mourning for some one of his family. He had taken from Master's effects his palette and brushes, saying that he wished to keep them near him. I was rather startled to see that he had them beside him on a chair as we spoke.

"Juan de Pareja," he said to me, "I once heard Don Diego, your late master, say that he had been tardy in giving you your freedom. It made him ashamed, and he repented bitterly of not having realized before that you had wanted and deserved your freedom long before he gave it."

"It is true that I longed for it, but not to leave him. Only because I wished to paint. I never held it against him that he had been forgetful."

"I know. And I know also how he felt. For I too have been remiss and tardy. Many a time it crossed my mind that I should name Don Diego a Knight of Santiago, but I never took the steps to do so. I let too much time go by and I blame myself. But I shall now name him to that high honor, and with your help we will paint on his bosom the red Cross of Santiago."

"But Sire, how . . . ?"

"Don Diego, to my knowledge, left only one self-portrait," said the King. "That is part of his wonderful picture, 'Las Meninas,' in which, by using mirrors, he made portraits of my Queen and my children and myself. We will go to that picture. Bring the palette and brushes."

We stood there looking at the picture. Master was at his easel, palette and brush in hand, but his eyes looked out toward us, thoughtfully, kindly.

"If you will help me . . . ," said the King.

I dipped the brush in the vermilion paint and put it into his hand. Then, guiding him, my brown hand holding that white hand of royalty, we traced the Cross of Santiago on Master's breast.

It was done.

I was glad that I had been able to do this last small service for him.

I do not remember much of those next few days, except that Lolis and I said good-by to our friends, to Master's little granddaughter (reminding me so much of Paquita at her age), and to Juan Bautista. For the last time we walked down Jeronimas Street and across the Plaza Mayor. I looked back at what had been home for me.

"Home for me, was where he was," I murmured.

Lolis took my hand.

"Home is where I am now, Husband," she said.

Fifteen

In which I find another home

SEVILLE was welcoming. The golden Giralda soared into the clear blue sky, the narrow streets were full of life, the shouting of softly slurred Spanish and much Arabic sounded in all the squares, and the Guadalquivir ran swiftly between its banks reflecting orange and olive trees, the white homes of Seville, and the dark, proud, spare and graceful figures of the southern people. In the cathedral the dear saints I had loved in my youth still looked down with tenderness upon me, and I knelt and prayed and breathed again the incense of my childhood.

Lolis and I had gone to an inn near the waterfront, one I had known about in the days when Don Basilio had worked there in his warehouses and when I had run errands for Doña Emilia. I walked about, grieving over some changes, but rejoicing to find so much the same. It is good to come full circle in one's life and, toward the end, turn back toward the beginnings.

I had some money. I had skills. I knew that I could work and earn a decent living as a free man.

But before I turned to the task of looking for a permanent home, I went to call on Bartolomé Esteban Murillo.

He himself opened the door when I knocked. He was the same—rotund, dark and smiling, full of good humor and kindness.

"Juan, my friend!" He embraced me and pulled me inside. It was full of noise. . . . A child was crying, others were shouting at their play, a dog barked happily in fun, and upstairs a woman was singing.

We talked at length in his studio, a big, not very tidy place, where five or six apprentices were busy copying religious works of Master Murillo himself.

I told him of the death of Paquita, and of Mistress. I spoke of Master's last days, and of how the King had painted the Cross of Santiago on the breast of his self-portrait.

"And what will you do now, my friend?"

"I was planning to look for a studio. . . ."

"Here you have one."

"I would love to work here with you, as in the old days. But my wife . . ."

"Bring her with you. We have lots of room. You must not be lonely in your first weeks here. Come to us, Juan! My children will wash your brushes for you! And, here with me, you can paint as much as you wish, in safety!"

I realized then that I had not yet told him that I was free. Yet he had taken me in and offered me his home and his studio.

I bowed my head and thanked him.

"I will go and bring Lolis," I told him, and as I went away toward the inn I thought about Bartolomé's generosity and candid comradeship. Some day, I thought, when we have finished work, and sit to take a glass of wine together—some day when our wives whispered and rocked children to sleep in the upper rooms—I would say, "Bartolomé, Master Velázquez freed me. I am no longer a slave."

And he would say, "So? Good, my friend."

He would be glad for me. And I would be glad that to him it had never mattered, for his friendship was of the heart.

Afterword

WHENEVER one tells a story about personages who actually lived, it becomes necessary to hang many invented incidents, characters, and events upon the thin thread of truth which has come down to us. The threads of the lives of Velázquez and Pareja are weak and broken; very little, for certain, is known about them.

Velázquez was a man who was unusually taciturn, even among painters, who do not distinguish themselves generally by writing very much or by leaving documents, letters and diaries. So far as we can tell, only one direct quotation can be authenticated, as from his lips, and it is significant, since he is now recognized as the precursor of the realistic, as well as of the impressionistic, school. "I would rather be first in painting something ugly than second in painting beauty," he said. Actually, the lack of "beautification" in his works is what makes them so evocative, so expressive, today; Velázquez was a man who loved truth, loved to paint it, and did not flatter himself that he could improve it.

It is known that Velázquez inherited Juan de Pareja from relatives in Seville; it is known that he gave him his freedom, and in the way in which my story sets it forth. It is known that the great portrait of Pareja was painted by Velázquez in Italy, at or about the time he painted Pope Innocent X.

Commentators say that Velázquez himself sent Pareja about with his own portrait in order to get commissions in Italy, but, judging from the affection which existed between the two men all their lives, I prefer to think that Pareja did his master this service, unknown to Velázquez. The portrait of Pareja shows a man intelligent, loyal, proud, and tender; the only self-portrait known of Velázquez (in "Las Meninas") shows detachment, sensitivity, sobriety. Biographies of many painters are constructed by scholars from a study of their works, plus known facts. In fiction, then, I think the author may be pardoned for making her own interpretations of some of the paintings that have come down to us over the centuries, Velázquez's only recorded "conversations."

Thus, I have chosen to believe that the lovely portrait titled "Lady with a Fan" was really Velázquez's daughter Francisca (Paquita), who married the painter Juan Bautista del Mazo, and I have suggested my own explanation of the little red flower which appears—nobody knows why—upon her skirt, just below the fold of her bodice.

It is true that slaves were not allowed to practice the arts in Spain, and I surmise that Pareja taught himself to paint in secret, for there is no doubt that he became an accomplished artist, and his canvases hang in several European museums.

Murillo did indeed work with Velázquez for some three years, in the Madrid studio. I assume that he was the tender, kindly, religious man his own canvases seem to reveal.

The incident of the visit to the religious image-maker I have based on the oft-told legend in Spain of the "Cristo de Limpias," a very beautiful crucifix, in which Christ is portrayed dying on the cross. It is said that a criminal was crucified (with his own consent), so as to supply the image-maker with a model in the very moments of agony.

Velázquez was knighted in 1658 by King Philip IV, yet it is known that the Cross of Santiago was painted on the bosom of the artist's self-portrait (in "Las Meninas") by some other hand after the painter's death—whose, history does not say. I would like to think this hand was the King's, guided by that of Juan de Pareja.

Facts of which I am certain are the bonds of deep respect and affection which united Velázquez to his sovereign, and, with equal strength, to his slave, whom he freed and named his assistant.

My story about Juan de Pareja will, I hope, be forgiven the liberties I have taken with known facts and the incidents I have invented. It will appeal, I hope, to young people of all races because the story of Juan de Pareja and Velázquez foreshadows, in the lifetime of the two men, what we hope to achieve a millionfold today. Those two, who began in youth as master and slave, continued as companions in their maturity and ended as equals and as friends.

Connected
Readings

from
The World of Velázquez

Dale Brown

AFTER Velázquez was put in charge of the construction of the Octagonal Room, his prestige at court reached new heights. The fact that he, rather than the Superintendent of Buildings, had won the job suggests that he had powerful friends close to the King—perhaps the Marquis of Eliche and his father, Haro. In the fall of 1648 Philip announced that he wanted to set up a new picture gallery and asked Velázquez to choose the artists to be represented there. Velázquez took immediate advantage of the situation to promote a scheme of his own. He saw no reason, he said, why the King should have pictures "like those anybody can have." He suggested that Philip grant him leave to travel again to Italy, this time "to search for and purchase the best pictures to be found"—paintings by Titian, Veronese, Raphael and others—as well as antique statues or casts. . . .

The painter was given 2,000 ducats for traveling expenses, and "the carriage due him because of his position." He elected to take with him an assistant, Juan de Pareja. Together they set sail from Málaga late in January 1649, traveling with a party of noblemen delegated to bring Philip's bride-to-be, the young Mariana, back to Spain. Arriving in Genoa in early March, Velázquez headed straight for Venice. Although 20 years had elapsed since his first visit there, the atmosphere was apparently still as openly hostile to Spaniards as it had been in 1629, and the greatest tact was required to get people to show Velázquez their paintings. The artist did, however, purchase several Tintorettos and Veronese's glorious *Venus and Adonis*.

From Venice Velázquez set off for Rome, making brief courtesy calls en route. At Modena the Duke whose portrait he had executed in 1638 made him promise to pay a return visit; at Bologna the Count of Siena and other dignitaries rode out in their coaches to welcome him, and the count put him up in his palace. Increasingly, Velázquez must have felt himself a personage—presumably he was receiving all these honors because of his status as a gentleman of Philip IV's court, not solely because of his artistic reputation.

119

He could not have picked a better time to be in Italy. Rome was preparing for the Jubilee celebration of 1650, which had been proclaimed by Pope Innocent X. Some 700,000 pilgrims would visit the Eternal City before the year was over—among them many of the great painters, architects and sculptors of Europe. Here Velázquez probably met the French master of classical painting, Poussin, and Bernini, the pioneer exponent of the baroque style.

But before Velázquez could settle down in Rome, he had first to go to Naples to collect the rest of his travel money from Philip's viceroy there. He took advantage of his visit to have casts made of antique sculptures for shipment back to Spain, and he may have called on his countryman, Ribera. As soon as he had attended to his business, he returned to Rome—there to remain for more than a year. His excitement must have run high. He was received by some of the city's leading citizens and patrons of the arts.

Rome seemed to unleash in Velázquez a burst of creative energy. In 17 or 18 months he painted at least 10 portraits and began several others. Five of the finished portraits survive: they are of Innocent X; the Pope's barber, who bore the illustrious name Michelangelo; Cardinal Astalli, the Pope's adopted nephew; Camillo Massimo, the Papal Chamberlain; and Juan de Pareja, Velázquez' assistant. He painted these, according to his early biographer Palomino, "with long-handled brushes, in Titian's vigorous manner." By using long-handled brushes, Velázquez could paint at some distance from his canvas without having to step back from his easel to gauge his effects and interrupt his creative flow. This technique would also have given him greater mobility and lent the pictures a sense of spontaneity. Certainly the vitality of his work was much admired by his fellow painters. "Superiority," wrote one, "consists in doing much with a few brushstrokes, freely executed so that the studied effect may appear spontaneous. This admirable method Diego Velázquez is now making famous, for with subtle skill, with a few strokes, he shows how much freedom of touch, and a rapid execution can accomplish."

As the art center of 17th Century Europe, Rome offered Velázquez the chance of a lifetime to show off his talent, and he lost little time in doing so. He became a member of the painters' guild in January 1650, and a few weeks later was admitted to a confederation of artists called the *Virtuosi al Pantheon,* a group that every March held a prestigious exhibition at the Pantheon, an ancient Roman temple. What won him almost instant recognition was the portrait of Pareja. He painted it as a kind of warming-up exercise for his portrait of the Pope, but apparently also with an eye to exhibiting it in the Pantheon show, where it was hung with works by his contemporaries and many of the great masters of the past. It is easy to see why the portrait brought Velázquez the applause of his fellow artists. The painting is a boldly executed work, and Pareja seems alive in it, his eyebrows arched, his eyes alert and shining. Many writers on Velázquez have referred to Pareja as his slave—presumably because Pareja was of Moorish ancestry—but one look at the painting is convincing evidence that a man as proud as this must have been free in spirit, if not in law.

The Angle of a Landscape—

Emily Dickinson

The Angle of a Landscape—
That every time I wake—
Between my Curtain and the Wall
Upon an ample Crack—

Like a Venetian—waiting—
Accosts my open eye—
Is just a Bough of Apples—
Held slanting, in the Sky—

The Pattern of a Chimney—
The Forehead of a Hill—
Sometimes—a Vane's Forefinger—
But that's—Occasional—

The Seasons—shift—my Picture—
Upon my Emerald Bough,
I wake—to find no—Emeralds—
Then—Diamonds—which the Snow

From Polar Caskets—fetched me—
The Chimney—and the Hill—
And just the Steeple's finger—
These—never stir at all—

The Boy Who Drew Sheep

Anne Rockwell

1

MORE than seven hundred years ago, in a valley in Italy, there lived a farmer named Bondone. He had a wife and a house, some pigs, a few cows, fig and olive trees, many, many woolly sheep, and a son to help him on the farm. The boy was named Giotto. When he was nine years old, his father entrusted the flock of sheep to him. Each morning, before the sun was up, Giotto and his dog led the sheep up into the hills where they nibbled all day at the meadow grass; and in the evening, when the moon rose, he led them safely home again.

Alone as he was, with no playmates or companions but his dog and sheep, Giotto began to pass the long days by scratching pictures with a sharp pebble on the large stones that jutted up here and there in the meadow. First he drew the things that came into his head, but after a while he decided to draw something that he had actually seen. And so he began to make a picture of one of his sheep. He worked and worked, but the drawing never seemed quite right. So when he finished one he would begin another. The time passed quickly this way, and wherever he wandered with his flock, the rocks were scratched with pictures of sheep: old and solemn rams, gentle ewes, and curly baby lambs.

One day a group of gentlemen on horseback came riding up into the hills where Giotto herded his flock. Both men and horses were dressed in the finest and shiniest silk and leather. Each gentleman carried a hawk on his wrist, and each hawk wore a little leather mask on his face. The men were hunting. But Giotto did not notice them, so busy was he with his newest drawing. Not far from where he sat, a little spring of fresh, cold water gushed up between two rocks. One of the gentlemen rode over all alone, and he and his horse drank from the cool water. While he was at the spring, he noticed the boy. So he walked quietly over and looked at the drawing.

Giotto must have been surprised to see the well-dressed stranger, for few people came into his hills. The gentleman introduced himself as Cimabue, a citizen of the city of Florence.

He congratulated Giotto on his fine drawing and said that he too was an artist. He painted pictures on the walls of the churches of Florence. The man looked again at Giotto's drawing and then offered to teach Giotto all of the many things he knew about picture painting. Giotto would have to come and work for him in his workshop, of course, if this were to happen. Giotto was surprised by this, for where he lived most men were farmers and shepherds, as their fathers had been and their sons would be, and there were no artists.

That evening, when the boy led the sheep back to the valley, Cimabue went with him. For a long time he spoke with Giotto's mother and father. He told them that of all the boys who had ever worked in his workshop (and there were many), none could draw so well, without any lessons, as their son Giotto.

The farmer Bondone was a practical man. He didn't want his son to waste his time in foolishness. But as he looked at the stranger's elegant clothes, which must have cost a great deal of money, he began to think that perhaps the stranger was right: Giotto should go and learn to paint pictures. Perhaps he too would grow rich. And so, before the family went to bed that night, it was settled. Giotto would go to Florence and become an apprentice in Cimabue's workshop.

2

EARLY next morning Giotto, instead of heading for the hills with his sheep, said good-bye to them and to his dog and to his mother and father. He climbed up in back of Cimabue on the painter's high-stepping horse, and the two of them set off toward Florence.

Many hours later they reached the gates of the city. Tall towers bristled proudly against the sky, and inside the strong walls were more people together than Giotto had seen in his whole life. Knights in armor rode through the busy streets; well-dressed merchants talked together of business; market stalls were filled to overflowing with sweet figs and melons and other good things from the hills.

On every corner, or so it seemed, women sat chatting and spinning wool into long skeins. Iron hooks projected from nearly all of the houses in Florence. Across these iron hooks lay cross-pieces of wood. And from these wooden cross-pieces hung great skeins of purple, crimson, gold, and deep blue wool, drying in the air. For the city of Florence was rich from wool, wool from the sheep that shepherds such as Giotto had raised in the hills. This good wool of Florence was sold to the world and the city's wool merchants were rich and proud.

The city was grand and glorious. Its churches were filled with pictures painted by artists such as Cimabue, artists all other cities in the world would have liked to have. The pictures covered the plaster walls of churches or hung from strong wooden panels. They gleamed with brilliant red and blue and paper-thin coatings of real gold, bright as the sun.

Cimabue took Giotto to the workshop, which stood on one of Florence's narrow, busy streets. There the boy was introduced to the other apprentices. Some of them were boys nearly as young as Giotto; others were almost men; and one or two were grown men without workshops of their own. They managed the workshop of Cimabue. The apprentices lived together behind the workshop. Giotto was welcomed as one of them, and his training began.

First he learned to make charcoal sticks for drawing. He cut up several willow switches into lengths just a little longer than his longest finger. Then he carefully sharpened each end to a point with his knife. Next he tied all of the willow sticks into several neat bundles. These bundles went into an earthenware casserole, with a cover. When the bundles were in, he sealed the cover of the casserole tight shut with a shaped piece of clay, so the inside was airtight. Last of all, he carefully carried the pot to the baker's shop. He gave it to the baker, who placed it at the entrance of one of the great ovens that he was lighting that night for the baking of fine loaves of bread early in the morning. And that night, all night long, the casserole sat in the baker's oven, while the boy slept and dreamed that the charcoal sticks would turn out well. For if the fire was too hot, or the willow bundles improperly packed, the charcoal would be too burnt, and it would crumble when it was put to paper or parchment. Then the boy who made it might be whipped. But if he was lucky and had done his work well, the sticks would be hard and black, and there would be charcoal for drawing for many weeks, and praise for him, too. When Giotto brought his first charcoal back to the workshop, he *was* lucky, for the sticks were perfect, black and sharp and crisp. He also brought breakfast . . . the first loaves of the morning, warm and round and crusty.

He learned to prepare parchment for drawing. From the leather tanner, pieces of skin from a very young calf were bought. These he washed, nailed to a wooden stretcher, and dried in the sunshine. Then, he picked up the chicken bones from under the dining table at night, where the apprentices threw them, and burned them in the fire until the ashes were white and soft. These ashes were ground on a smooth stone slab until they were even softer. Then, with a furry rabbit's foot, he dusted the powder back and forth, back and forth across the dried skin until it was velvet smooth and ready to take the lines made by charcoal, or if more delicate work was wanted, by a little piece of tarnished silver wire from the goldsmith's workshop.

And all the time he was learning these things, Giotto, in the little time he had left for himself, drew pictures . . . just as he had while he tended his father's sheep in the high hills.

3

SOMETIMES the other apprentices told him stories of the glory that came to a painter as skilled and admired as their master. Once Cimabue had received a commission to paint a picture of the Virgin Mary. She was to be surrounded by angels, and she would sit against a sky of gold. The picture would hang in a church in Florence in a spot where all would see it, including the visiting foreign kings and princes who came to Florence. It was springtime when Cimabue began the painting. One day the breezes blew so soft and pleasant, and the air smelled so sweetly of violets, that Cimabue moved his easel outdoors to his garden to paint. A neighbor, watching from a window, saw the picture and passed the word to a friend that it was more beautiful than anyone could possibly imagine. Word spread through the city, and next morning, when Cimabue came out to paint, many many people were already peeping over his garden wall to watch him while he worked. Even the king of France, who happened to be passing through Florence, joined the citizens as they stood and watched.

"How beautiful!" everyone said, as Cimabue painted in an apple-pink cheek.

"How glorious!" they said, as he burnished the gold-leaf background with the smooth tooth of an ox, until the gold was dark and shining.

When the painting was done, the citizens nearly wept with joy at the sight of it; and they decided that a picture as special as this one needed as special a journey as possible to the church where it was to hang. And so on the day the painting made its journey from the workshop to the church, it was accompanied by a grand parade of fifers, tambour drummers and trumpeters—and by everyone in the city, or so it seemed. Every apprentice hoped that such fame would one day come to him. Every young painter hoped that one day he would make pictures as fine as the pictures of Cimabue.

But for Giotto it was enough for now to draw and to hope that one day his master would say, "Here Giotto, paint in the face of this angel—the one in the far-left corner." Giotto worked, and he drew, and he lived the life of an apprentice.

4

AT the time Giotto lived, in the city of Florence as in other cities, only the boys of the rich went to school. All other boys learned a trade. They were apprenticed to master craftsmen, who provided food, clothing and shelter, as well as learning. In return the boys worked for the master.

In Florence there was a strange custom that Giotto must have enjoyed. Each day when noontime came, all of the apprentices from all of the trades in the city left their workshops and ran to the marketplace for lunch. There they feasted on sausages and fresh figs, and drank cool sweet lemonade from the lemon vendor's stall faster than the poor man could squeeze it. But sometimes fights broke out between apprentices: the wool-dyers fought with the painters; the carpenters fought with the apothecaries; the goldsmiths fought with the sculptors; for each trade thought its own best. At times like that the market ran wild, and geese ran cackling shrilly underfoot; stall-keepers shouted vainly to the boys to stop while onions and lemons turned to weapons and went flying through the air. But suddenly the market bell would clang out loudly over the shouting and swearing, and the apprentices would return to work, always promising to finish the fight the next day. As they left, the unfortunate stall-keepers would sigh and swear and once more pile their goods neat and high.

Back at the workshop, Giotto and his fellow apprentices would dig into their work, having had their fling for the day. In Cimabue's workshop the apprentices were treated kindly. Although they worked hard, they ate well and slept in clean and comfortable beds.

But there were some painters who treated their apprentices badly and made them work too hard. One old painter, a stingy man, had but one apprentice, who was as lazy as his master was stingy. Each morning, in the cold darkness before dawn, the master woke the apprentice and set him hard at work grinding colors, preparing panels of wood and making brushes; then when day came the master could paint angels, although, to tell the truth, his angels were not beautiful. The lazy apprentice so hated waking up while it was still dark and shivery that he made up his mind to put a stop to it. Since he was not only lazy but an untidy housekeeper, in all corners of the workshop and under every piece of furniture, dust lay thick. Little creepy beetles lived in the dust. And one night while his master slept, the apprentice caught many, many of these little beetles. With a tiny dripping of wax, he fastened a very small candle to each beetle's back. Then, after lighting each candle, he set the beetle army loose in his master's bedroom and hid in the hall. As the beetles slowly proceeded across the floor, like a long, silent, flaming dragon, the old painter wakened and shouted and screamed in terror, while the apprentice sat outside giggling silently. When morning came, the painter, in a trembling voice, told the apprentice of the terrible thing that had happened in the night.

"I am sure," he said, "that those were demons come to get me. They are very angry because I have been painting so many angels, for angels are good and demons are bad! But the night belongs to strange monsters! Let us leave it to them; from now on we work no more until the sun, which chases away demons, is fully up in the morning."

And so it was that the lazy apprentice could sleep late in the morning. Indeed in all the workshops of Florence, everyone heard of the flaming demons and took heed; and from that time on, work was done only in daylight hours.

That did not stop apprentices from playing other tricks, however. Giotto, too, invented some. He was now allowed to paint small portions of the master's canvases himself. One day he painted a tiny fly on the nose of a figure on a panel. He giggled as his master tried unsuccessfully to brush it off, for he thought it was real. And although Cimabue would not admit it, the boy's joke also gave him pleasure, for it showed that the young shepherd from the hills was learning his trade remarkably well.

But there was much more to being a painter than painting a fly to fool the eye. Giotto had to make brushes, delicate brushes of ermine tails for small and precise work, and hard strong bristle brushes made from the back hairs of a white pig for more general work. He learned to grind the priceless chunks of color that he had gotten from the apothecary shop. He would grind and grind until they seemed to be as fine as dust; but then, when he showed them to his master, they would still be too coarse.

"Grind them," the master would say, "until you are sure you have ground them enough, and then grind them some more."

And so he would grind them again, and then again. But at last they would be ready and he would place them in neat little pots. There were all of the colors. Some were made of ground-up stones or earth, and some were products of the mysterious arts of the alchemist. Some behaved strangely when mixed with other colors and therefore had to be used pure. There were still others that were highly poisonous. All of the rules for the use of all of the colors had to be learned before a painter could be sure that his pictures would not turn black in a short time.

Even worse, a painter who was careless of the way he handled some of the paint could develop symptoms of poisoning. He must not lick his brushes to make a point for delicate work. He must not inhale too much of the finely ground colored dust before it was mixed with water or oil or egg white to make it ready to spread on a picture.

The craft of a painter was filled with things that seemed magical and mysterious to those who had not learned the craft. And the images that grew on walls and panels, with blue made of precious ground lapis lazuli and reds of rare and rich cinnabar from Spain, and bright gold gleaming, seemed magical and mysterious to those who looked at them. But Giotto was now a part of those mysteries. He was becoming a painter.

5

THE years passed, and the boy Giotto grew up. Wherever he went he looked at people and at the world around him. He noticed the way people stood and moved in the busy marketplace, and he noticed the way they looked when they laughed or cried. He watched the way the long drapery of their clothing fell in rich folds to the ground when they walked or gestured. And always he drew what he saw, as he had done up in the hills. But now it was different, for he had learned so many things that he could draw well whatever he wished. He had mastered all of the many skills he needed to be a painter with a workshop of his own. Indeed, there were many people who said that he surpassed his master, the most famous painter in the land.

Giotto was soon called upon by the neighboring town of Assisi to paint some pictures for them.

Nearly one hundred years earlier a man called Francis had been born in Assisi. He was the son of a rich merchant, but he gave up all of his money and fine clothes and called himself, "the Little Poor Man." As a beggar, he wandered throughout Italy doing good things. Not only did he love people, but he loved the sun and moon as if they were his brother and sister, and he loved all of the birds and creatures of the earth. He even seemed able to speak to wild animals in their own language. He wrote poems and songs in praise of the wild things of the earth. These were written in the language the people around him spoke every day, instead of the Latin of learned poets. He wanted to teach people to live together more happily, and at the same time he wanted to teach them to share the earth with the birds and flowers, wild wolves, and fire and water and cold winter wind. After he died he became known as Saint Francis, and his native town wished to honor him by building a church dedicated to him. Giotto was asked to decorate the church with murals, telling stories from the life of Saint Francis. And so Giotto journeyed to Assisi to begin the work.

First, carpenters constructed a strong wooden scaffolding where he could stand with his assistants to reach the high walls where they would make the paintings. Next the bare stone walls were covered with a rough coat of plaster. Upon this plaster Giotto drew with charcoal, carefully copying and enlarging a small picture he had drawn previously on paper. Then he went over the charcoal with a little brush and brown paint, until the whole picture could easily be seen on the plaster. When he was ready to begin the finished painting, he mixed a small amount of fine smooth plaster and covered with it just enough of the wall with the picture drawn on for one day's work. While the plaster was still wet, although set, he painted the parts of the picture that were in that area, using his dry colors mixed with water. The next day he again plastered a small area and painted it, generally the section adjoining the section he had finished the day before. Day after day he worked in this way. Many, many months passed, or perhaps longer, before the murals were done.

Then at last, there they stood, row after row of grand and bright paintings. Scenes from the life of Saint Francis covered the walls like pages from an enormous picture book for people to see, many of whom could neither read nor write.

These paintings were not like any that people had seen before. The pictures people of Giotto's time knew were stiff and unreal, painted in a way handed down from master to apprentice for hundreds of years. They looked more like other pictures than they looked like real life. But Giotto, like Saint Francis, had looked at the world around him and had seen that it was beautiful. He painted trees and animals, prickly plants and meadow flowers, strong boulders and tall city walls. But what was most unusual was the way he painted people. He filled many spaces with people, people who moved and smiled and cried and gestured as real people do, but who were larger than life. People loved what they saw in Giotto's pictures, but when they looked at him, they laughed, for they said he was as small and ugly as his pictures were large and beautiful.

From city to city Giotto went, climbing scaffoldings and covering wall after wall with pictures. One day after painting many pictures in many cities, he was walking down a narrow alley in Florence, chatting with a friend. He did not notice a runaway pig escaping from the butcher's stall in the marketplace. Squealing shrilly, the pig took one look at Giotto, headed straight toward him and darted between the painter's legs, tripping him up, head over heels. As he pulled himself up and brushed the dirt from his clothes, Giotto laughed and said, "That pig must have known I am the painter who has used so many of his brothers' back bristles for brushes. I have made a great deal of money with my pig-bristle brushes, but I have never given a pig even a bowl of leftovers. Now, at last, I have paid my debt to pigs!"

6

IN the city of Padua there had lived a man called Scrovegni. He was a wicked man who loaned money to people and then charged such high rates of interest that they could not pay, and sometimes had to forfeit land or goods instead. When he died, he was very rich, but he was hated, by all who had heard of him, for his greed and cruelty. His son decided to use his father's great wealth to build a fine church for the city, so that his father would be remembered for this instead of for his crimes. The son commissioned Giotto, who was by then more famous than Cimabue or any painter had ever been, to cover the walls of the new church with scenes from the life of Jesus. Some say that Giotto even helped the stonemasons plan the church, to make certain that he had plenty of wall space for his pictures. The son of the thief had planned well, for today people come from all over the world to look at Giotto's pictures, and the Scrovegni family is still remembered for the beautiful paintings in the chapel that bears its name.

One day a messenger came to Giotto from far-away Avignon, in France. This was the city where the Pope lived at that time. The messenger had been sent to many artists in Italy, all of the best painters, to ask them to submit a painting for a contest. The prize would be a chance to do some well-paid work in Avignon. All of the artists the messenger approached worked very hard on their samples for the contest. But when the messenger asked Giotto for his picture, Giotto took a piece of charcoal and, resting his elbow on the table, with no compass to guide him, drew a perfect circle.

"Is this all I am to take?" cried the astonished messenger, when Giotto gave him the drawing of the circle.

And Giotto answered, smiling, that it was. But the Pope, looking at all of the pictures the artists had labored hard over, liked none of them. Not until he came to the perfect circle did he tell the messenger that he had, at last, found the man he wanted. The job went to Giotto. What it was, we shall never know, for the painting is gone today, but people still speak of something as being as simple as Giotto's "O."

Giotto went to Naples and painted for the king of that area. The king loved to watch the painter work and spent many hours doing just that. One hot day, as Giotto stood high on his scaffolding, without a breeze in the air, the king, who was resting below, eating cool and juicy fruits, called lazily up to him, "Ahhhhhh . . . Giotto . . . if I were you, I would not work on such a day as this!"

Giotto laughed and answered, "No, your majesty, I would not work either, if I were *you!*"

For it was hard work to be a painter. Besides the wonderful murals, which brought painters fame and wealth, there was other work for them to do. They painted coats of arms on shields, decorated bridal chests and floats for parades and festivals. And not only did they paint and design the floats, they even painted the faces of the ladies and children who rode on them, so that they might appear as pink-cheeked and rosy-lipped as angels.

As his father on the farm, long years before, had hoped, Giotto became very rich. He married and had eight children, each one, so it was said, as homely as himself. He trained many apprentices in his workshop, and one, named Taddeo Gaddi, he adopted as his own son.

The days passed, and slowly Giotto grew to be an old man. But still he painted. He was hard at work one day when some citizens of Florence came to him and asked him to design a bell tower for the city. Although Giotto was no architect, he felt this was a great honor, and he agreed to do it. He began work at once on plans and designs for the bell tower. On it he decided to put as many of the people he had seen in his long life as he could. There would be pictures of all the different trades men followed: farming and fishing, weaving and building, masonry, carpentry and wool-dying. He did not forget the sheep, the sheep he had first looked at as he learned to draw. In a shepherd's tent a man sat, guarding three nibbling sheep. A wag-tailed dog stood nearby to help. To Giotto this represented the first herdsman in all the world. One panel, too, was for the painters. There a man stood patiently and intently at work upon a panel, his well-ground colors near him in a row of little pots.

The drawings Giotto made were copied in stone by sculptors to decorate the sides of the bell tower. Huge wooden scaffoldings were built, far stronger than any that were needed for a painter, and the work on the tall stone tower was begun. For three years Giotto worked on this and nothing else. He drew and planned and directed the stonemasons and carpenters. And the tower grew and grew.

But Giotto never saw it stand tall and proud and finished. In 1337, when he was seventy-one years old, he died, and the tower was not yet done. But today, when its bell rings out across the city and up into the hills where he wandered as a shepherd boy so long ago, people say,

"The bells are ringing on Giotto's tower."

Stone Carving in Kotzebue

Jim Schoppert

I held the stone
and logic ruled the stroke
of knife
upon that stone.

Shadows
cast by striking light
determined depth of cut
and nuance,
and through it all—

the constant
fingering of the cuts;
the deliberate turning
in my hands to better see
the work progress—

a subtle nature
was revealed.

from

My Name Is Asher Lev

Chaim Potok

My Name Is Asher Lev *is the fictional autobiography of a boy named Asher Lev who lives in Brooklyn, New York. Driven by his exceptional artistic talent and his intense awareness of the world around him, Asher chooses to draw and paint everything he sees. Although his decision to pursue art challenges the views of his parents and his Orthodox Jewish community, for Asher, painting is not merely something he does, it is something he must do. This excerpt describes the initial reactions of Asher's uncle and father to his extraordinary artistic ability.*

MY father's brother came over to our apartment sometime before Passover. He was about five years older than my father, short, somewhat portly, with a round dark-bearded face, watery brown eyes, and full moist lips that collected spittle at the corners when he spoke. He operated a successful jewelry and watch-repair store on Bedford Avenue, a few blocks from where we lived. He had two sons and two daughters and lived in a two-story brownstone on President Street.

We sat in the living room. The window was partly open. The Venetian blind swayed faintly in the breeze that blew into the room.

My father's brother wanted us to join his family in his home for the Passover sedorim. My father thanked him but would not accept.

"Why?"

"Rivkeh cannot leave the apartment. We'll have the sedorim here."

"Alone?"

"Yes."

My uncle squinted his watery eyes. "Listen," he said. "I don't want to mix into your affairs, but I'm your brother, and if a brother can't mix, who can? Have you talked to the Rebbe?"

"No."

"You should talk to the Rebbe."

My father looked at his hands and said nothing.

"Don't look away from me like that. Listen to me. I know how you feel about such things. But when our father had trouble he went to the Rebbe's father. I remember. You were only a baby. But I remember."

"It's not yet time to go to the Rebbe."

"What does the doctor say?"

"The doctor doesn't say anything anymore."

"Then it's time. Believe me, it's time. What are you waiting for? People go to the Rebbe because they have a cold."

"I'm not such people."

"Listen to me. You should talk to the Rebbe."

"The Rebbe has a thousand problems."

"Then one more can't hurt. Listen to an older brother. Talk to the Rebbe."

At that point, my father asked me to leave. I went to my room, sat at my desk, and drew pictures of my uncle. I made him very round and dark-bearded, and I gave him a kind smile and warm eyes. He always wore dark-blue suits, but I made his suit light blue because he did not feel dark blue to me.

I was working on the third picture of my uncle when he and my father came into my room. They stood behind me. My uncle peered over my shoulder at the drawings.

"This is a six-year-old boy?" he said softly.

My father said nothing.

"A little Chagall," my uncle said.

I felt more than saw my father make a motion with his hands and head.

"I fix watches and sell jewelry," my uncle said. "But I have eyes."

"Who is Chagall?" I asked.

"A great artist," my uncle said.

"Is he the greatest artist in the world?"

"He is the greatest Jewish artist in the world."

"Who is the greatest artist?"

My uncle thought a moment. "Picasso," he said.

"Picasso," I said, tasting the name. "Picasso. Is Picasso American?"

"Picasso is Spanish. But he lives in France."

"What does Picasso look like?" I asked.

My uncle pursed his lips and squinted his eyes. "He is short and bald and has dark burning eyes."

"How do you know about such things?" my father asked.

"I read. A watchmaker does not necessarily have to be an ignoramus."

"It's late," my father said to me. "Get into your pajamas, Asher. I'll come back to put you to sleep."

"A regular Chagall," my uncle said.

I turned in my chair and looked up at him. "No," I said. "My name is Asher Lev."

The two of them stared at me for a moment. My father's mouth dropped open a little. My uncle laughed softly.

"This is six years old?" he said. "Good night, Asher." Then he said, "I want to buy one of these drawings. Will you sell it to me for this?"

He took a coin from his pocket and showed it to me. He picked up one of the drawings and put the coin in its place. "Now I own an early Lev," he said, with a smile.

I did not understand what he was saying. I looked at my father. His face was dark.

"Good night, Asher," my uncle said.

They went out of the room.

The coin gleamed in the light of the lamp on my desk. I could not understand what had happened. I found myself suddenly missing the drawing and afraid to touch the coin. I wanted the drawing back.

My father came into the room. He held the drawing in his hand. Without a word, he put it on the desk and took the coin. He was angry.

"Your Uncle Yitzchok has a strange sense of humor," he said, and went from my room.

I looked at the drawing. I felt happy to have it back. But I felt unhappy my uncle had not kept it. It was a strange feeling. I could not understand it.

My father returned to the room. "I asked you to get into pajamas," he said.

I began to undress. He sat on my bed, watching me. He did not offer to help.

"Is my papa angry?" I asked when I came back from the bathroom.

"Your papa's tired," he said. Then he said, "Asher, would you like to go to Uncle Yitzchok for the sedorim?"

"Will you and Mama be with me?"

"Your mama can't leave the house."

"I want to be with you and Mama."

He sighed softly and was silent a moment. Then he shook his head. "Master of the Universe," he said in Yiddish. "What are You doing?"

The weather turned warm. Green buds appeared on the trees. The sun shone into the living room through the huge window. The rug and white walls and furniture shimmered with light. The light seemed to have a life of its own. On Shabbos and Sunday afternoons, when my father did not go to his office, I stayed in the living room and watched the sunlight. I watched the colors change. I watched new shapes come alive and die in the slow movement of color and light. Sometimes my eyes would hurt after a day of watching.

My mother began to sit in the living room in the sunlight. She sat on the sofa near the window, her eyes closed, sunlight bathing her face. She rarely moved once she sat down on the sofa. Her skin was sallow, translucent. She seemed drained of substance, dry skin and brittle bones surrounding empty space.

One Sunday afternoon, I brought my pencil and pad into the living room and drew my mother sitting on the sofa. I drew the sagging curve of her shoulders and back, the concave depression of her chest, the bony stalks of her arms crossed on her lap, the tilt of her head resting against a shoulder with the sun full on her eyes. She did not appear to be bothered by the sun. It was as if there were nothing behind her eyes for the sun to bother.

I was having trouble with her face. The cheek on the left side of her face dropped sharply into a concave plane from the high ridge of bone. I could not do the shading with the pencil. There were gradations of darkness in the shade which the pencil could not capture. I tried it once and it did not work. I used the eraser. Then I tried it again and used the eraser again, and now the drawing was smudged; some of the line had been weakened. I put it away and on a new piece of paper once again drew the outer contour of my mother's body and the inner contour of her arms. I left the face blank for a while, then filled in the eyes and nose and mouth. I did not want to use the pencil again. The drawing felt incomplete. It bothered me to have it incomplete. I closed my eyes and looked at the drawing inside myself, went over its contours inside myself, and it was incomplete. I opened my eyes. Along the periphery of my vision, I saw the ashtray on the table next to the sofa. It was filled with my mother's smoked-out cigarettes. I looked at the crushed dark ends of the cigarettes. Quietly I went to the ashtray and brought it to my chair. I put it on the floor. Then, holding the pad with the drawing on my lap, I carefully brushed the burnt end of a cigarette onto my mother's face. The ash left an ugly smudge. I rubbed the smudge with my pinkie. It spread smoothly, leaving a gray film. I used the ash from another cigarette. The gray film deepened. I worked a long time. I used cigarette ash on the part of her shoulder not in sunlight and on the folds of her housecoat. The contours of her body began to come alive. I was working on the shadows in the sockets of her eyes when I realized that my father was in the room watching me.

I had no idea how long he had been standing in the doorway. But from the way he was leaning against the wall near the doorway I thought he had been there a long time. He was not looking at me but at the drawing. He could see the drawing clearly from where he stood. There were fascination and perplexity on his face. He seemed awed and angry and confused and dejected, all at the same time.

I thought he would be angry at me for drawing my mother while she rested. Instead he simply turned and went quietly from the room. I heard him walk up the hallway and go into his bedroom.

I put the ashtray back on the table near the sofa, collected my pad and pencil, and went to my room.

That night, as my father helped me out of my clothes, he said quietly, "I wish you wouldn't spend all your time playing with pencils and crayons, Asher."

"It isn't playing, Papa. It's drawing."

"I wish you wouldn't spend all your time drawing," my father said.

"Is my papa angry with me for drawing my mama this afternoon?"

"No," he said wearily. "No."

"I was careful not to wake my mama."

"I saw."

"Mama didn't wake up."

"Who showed you to use cigarettes that way?"

"I thought of it by myself. Once I used sand in a drawing and I thought of it by myself, too. It was when I went rowing with Mama."

My father was silent a long moment. He seemed very tired.

"Did I give you your vitamins today, Asher?"

"Yes, Papa."

He turned off the light. "Let me hear your Krias Shema."

I recited the Krias Shema. He kissed me and started slowly from the room.

"Papa?"

"Yes, Asher."

"I'm sorry for drawing Mama and making you angry at me."

He started to say something, then stopped.

"I wanted to draw the light and the dark," I said.

"Yes," he said softly. "Go to sleep, Asher."

He went from the room.

I'll have to draw it again, I thought. Maybe there is something else besides cigarettes I can use. It's too hard to work with cigarettes. And they smell. There must be something else. I fell asleep. I dreamed of my father's great-great-grandfather. He was dozing in the sunlight in the living room and I was drawing him, when he woke. He went into a rage. He stormed about the room. He was huge. He towered over me. His dark beard cast huge swaying shadows across the rug. "Wasting time, wasting time," he thundered. "Playing, drawing, wasting time." I woke in terror, my heart beating loudly. I lay in bed and could not sleep. I went to the bathroom. . . .On the way to my room, I saw a dim light in the living room. I looked in. My father stood near the window, swaying back and forth. I went silently back to my bed. I would find something other than cigarettes. I would put all the world into light and shade, bring life to all the wide and tired world. It did not seem an impossible thing to do.

A Time of Beginnings

Jade Snow Wong

AFTER Jade Snow began working in Mr. Fong's window, which confined her clay spatters, her activity revealed for the first time to Chinatown residents an art which had distinguished Chinese culture. Ironically, it was not until she was at college that she became fascinated with Tang and Sung Dynasty[1] achievements in clay, a thousand years ago.

Her ability to master pottery made her father happy, for Grandfather Wong believed that a person who could work with his hands would never starve. When Father Wong was young, Grandfather made him learn how to hand-pierce and stitch slipper soles, and how to knot Chinese button heads, both indispensable in clothing. But to Mother Wong, the merits of making pottery escaped her—to see her college-educated daughter up to her elbows in clay, and more clay flying around as she worked in public view, was strangely unladylike. As for Chinatown merchants, they laughed openly at her, "Here comes the girl who plays with mud. How many bowls could you sell today?" Probably they thought: Here is a college graduate fool ish enough to dirty her hands.

It has been the traditional belief from Asia to the Middle East, with Japan the exception, that scholars do not soil their hands and that a person studied literature in order to escape hard work. (This attitude is still prevalent in most Asian countries outside of the People's Republic of China and Japan.)

From the first, the local Chinese were not Jade Snow's patrons. The thinness and whiteness of porcelains imported from China and ornate decorations which came into vogue during the late Ching Dynasty[2] satisfied their tastes. They could not understand why "silly Americans" paid dollars for a hand-thrown bowl[3] utilizing crude California colored clays, not much different from the inexpensive peasant ware of China. That the

---

[1]**Tang and Sung** (sooŋ) **Dynasty:** A dynasty is a succession of rulers who belong to the same family. The period of the Tang Dynasty was 618–906 and that of the Sung Dynasty 960–1279.
[2]**Ching Dynasty:** This dynasty lasted from 1644 to 1912.
[3]**hand-thrown bowl:** A bowl shaped by hand on a potter's wheel, which spins the clay around.

Jade Snow Wong bowl went back to an older tradition of understated beauty was not apparent. They could see only that she wouldn't apply a dragon or a hundred flowers.

Many years later when Jade Snow met another atypical artist, a scholar and calligrapher[4] born and educated in China, he was to say to her, "I shudder if the majority of people look at my brush work and say it is pretty, for then I know it is ordinary and I have failed. If they say they do not understand it, or even that it is ugly, I am happy, for I have succeeded."

However, there were enough numbers of the American public who bought Jade Snow's pottery to support her modestly. The store window was a temporary experiment which proved what she needed to know. In the meantime, her aging father, who was fearful that their home and factory might be in a redevelopment area, made a down payment with lifetime savings to purchase a small white wooden building with six rentable apartments at the perimeter of Chinatown. Jade Snow agreed to rent the two tiny empty ground-floor storefronts which he did not yet need, one for a display room, with supplies and packing center at its rear, the other for the potter's wheel, kiln[5], glazing booth[6], compressor,[7] and other equipment. Now, instead of paying Mr. Fong a commission on gross sales, she had bills to pay. Instead of sitting in a window, she worked with doors thrown open to the street.

Creativeness was 90 percent hard work and 10 percent inspiration. It was learning from errors, either from her lack of foresight or because of the errors of others. The first firing[8] in an unfamiliar new gas kiln brought crushing disappointment when the wares blew up into tiny pieces. In another firing, glaze results were uneven black and dark green, for the chemical supply house had mistakenly labeled five pounds of black copper oxide as black iron oxide. One morning there was a personal catastrophe. Unaware of a slow leak all night from the partially opened gas cock, she lit a match at the kiln. An explosion injured both hands, which took weeks to heal.

The day-to-day work of potterymaking tested her deepest discipline. A "wedged" ball of clay (prepared by kneading) would be

---

[4]**calligrapher** (kə lig′ rə fər) *n.*: Someone skilled in the art of beautiful handwriting.
[5]**kiln** (kiln) *n.*: An oven to bake pottery.
[6]**glazing booth:** A place to apply glaze, a glassy finish, to pottery.
[7]**compressor** (kəm pres′ ər) *n.*: A machine for compressing air or gas.
[8]**firing** (fir′ iŋ) *n.*: The application of heat to harden or glaze pottery.

"thrown" (shaped) on the potter's wheel, then dried overnight and trimmed, sometimes decorated with Chinese brush or bamboo tools. It took about a hundred thoroughly dried pieces to fill a kiln for the first firing that transformed fragile mud walls into hard bisque ware.[9] Glazes, like clays the results of countless experiments, were then applied to each piece. A second twelve-hour firing followed, with the temperatures raised hour by hour up to the final maturing point of somewhere around 2,000 degrees Fahrenheit. Then the kiln was turned off for twenty-four hours of cooling. Breakage was a potential hazard at every stage; each step might measure short in technical and artistic accomplishment. A piece she worked on diligently could disappoint. Another made casually had been enhanced successively until it delighted. One piece in ten might be of exhibition quality, half might be salable, and the others would be flawed "seconds" she would discard.

Yet Jade Snow never wavered from her belief that if moments in time could result in a thing of beauty that others could share, those moments were immeasurably satisfying. She owned two perfect Sung tea bowls. Without copying, she tried to make her pottery "stand up" in strength and grace to that standard.

It became routine to work past midnight without days off. Hand work could not be rushed; failures had to be replaced, and a host of other unanticipated business chores suddenly manifested themselves. She had kept comparable hours when she worked all through college to meet her expenses. Again, the hope of reaching valued goals was her spur. If she should fail, then she could accept what tradition dictated for most Chinese daughters—to be a wife, daughter-in-law, and mother. But unlike her college, the American business world was not dedicated to helping her. Because she was pioneering in a new venture, her identity was a liability. Her brains and hands were her only assets. How could she convert that liability? How could she differ from other struggling potters?

To enlarge her production base, she experimented with enamels[10] on copper forms conceived in the fluid shapes of her pottery, layering jewel tones for brilliant effects. They differed from the earth tints of clay and attracted a new clientele. With another kiln and new equipment, she made functional forms,

---

[9]**bisque** (bisk) **ware:** Unglazed pottery.
[10]**enamels** (i nam″ls) *n.:* Glassy colored substances used as coatings on metal, glass, and pottery.

believing that fine things should become part of the user's everyday life. The best results were submitted to exhibitions. Some juries rejected them, some accepted, and others awarded prizes.

To reach a market larger than San Francisco, she wrote to store buyers around the country, and, encouraged, she called on them. Traveling to strange cities far across the United States, as a rare Oriental woman alone in hotel dining rooms, she developed strong nerves against curious stares. That trip produced orders. Stipulated delivery and cancellation dates made it necessary to hire first one and then more helpers who had to be trained, checked, kept busy and happy.

The strains increased. So did the bills, and she borrowed in small amounts from her sympathetic father, who said, "A hundred dollars is easy to come by, but the first thousand is very, very tricky. Look at the ideograph[11] for hundred—solidly square. Look at it for thousand—pointed, slippery. The ancients knew this long ago." When hundreds were not enough, tactful Western friends offered help. Oldest Brother, noticing her worries and struggles, sniffed scornfully. "You'll be out of business in a year."

She had learned to accept family criticism in silence, but she was too deeply involved to give up. Money was a worry, but creating was exciting and satisfying. These were lonely years. Jade Snow's single-minded pursuit did not allow her pleasant interludes with friends. To start a kiln at dawn, then watch till its critical maturing moment, which could happen any time between early evening and midnight or later (when gas pressure was low, it took until the next dawn), kept her from social engagements.

Then, gradually, signs indicated that she was working in the right direction. The first was a letter from the Metropolitan Museum of Art in New York, where the Eleventh Ceramic National Syracuse Show had been sent. The curator wrote, "We think the green, gold and ivory enamel bowl a skillful piece of workmanship and are anxious to add it to our collections." They referred to a ten-inch shallow bowl which Jade Snow had made.

A reviewer in *Art Digest* wrote, "In plain enamels without applied design, Jade Snow Wong of San Francisco seemed to this critic to top the list."

---

[11]**ideograph** (idē ə graf´) *n.*: A symbol that stands for a thing or idea without expressing the sounds that make up its name.

148

Recognition brought further recognition. National decorating magazines featured her enamels, and in the same year, 1947, the Museum of Modern Art installed an exhibit by Mies Van der Rohe[12] which displayed 100 objects of fine design costing less than $100. A note introducing this exhibit read, "Every so often the Museum of Modern Art selects and exhibits soundly designed objects available to American purchasers in the belief that this will encourage more people to use beautiful things in their everyday life. . . ." Two of Jade Snow's enamels, a dinner plate in Chinese red and a dessert plate in grayish gold, were included in the exhibition, which subsequently went to Europe.

So it did not seem unusual to receive an interviewer from *Mademoiselle*, but it was indeed unexpected to receive one of the magazine's ten awards for 1948 to women outstanding in ten different fields. They invited Jade Snow to fly to New York to claim her silver medal.

The more deeply one delves into a field, the more one realizes limitations. When Bernard Leach, the famous English potter, accepted an invitation from Mills College to teach a special course, Jade Snow attended. Another summer, Charles Merritt came from Alfred University's staff to give a course in precise glaze chemistry. Again, she commuted to Oakland. She became friends with these two unusual teachers. Both agreed that in pottery making, one never found a final answer. A mass-produced bathtub may be a technical triumph; yet a chemically balanced glaze on a pot can be aesthetically dull. Some of the most pleasing glaze effects could never be duplicated, for they were the combination of scrapings from the glaze booth. Like the waves of the sea, no two pieces of pottery art can be identical.

After three years of downs, then ups, the business promised to survive. Debts had been cleared. A small staff could handle routine duties. A steady clientele of San Franciscans came to her out-of-the-way shop. A beginning had been made.

---

[12]**Mies Van der Rohe** (mēz′ van dər rō′ə): Ludwig Mies Van der Rohe (1886–1969) was a German-born American architect.

Large Bad Picture

Elizabeth Bishop

Remembering the Strait of Belle Isle or
some northerly harbor of Labrador,
before he became a schoolteacher
a great-uncle painted a big picture.

Receding for miles on either side
into a flushed, still sky
are overhanging pale blue cliffs
hundreds of feet high,

their bases fretted by little arches,
the entrances to caves
running in along the level of a bay
masked by perfect waves.

On the middle of that quiet floor
sits a fleet of small black ships,
square-rigged, sails furled, motionless,
their spars like burnt match-sticks.

And high above them, over the tall cliffs'
semi-translucent ranks,
are scribbled hundreds of fine black birds
hanging in n's in banks.

One can hear their crying, crying,
the only sound there is
except for occasional sighing
as a large aquatic animal breathes.

In the pink light
the small red sun goes rolling, rolling,
round and round and round at the same height
in perpetual sunset, comprehensive, consoling,
while the ships consider it.
Apparently they have reached their destination.
It would be hard to say what brought them there,
commerce or contemplation.

The Wife's Portrait

Keigo Seki

VERY, very long ago in a certain place there lived a rather slow-witted man named Gombei. He became thirty, then forty years old, but there was no one who would become his wife. He lived all alone in a dirty little hut.

One evening a beautiful woman, such as he had never seen before, came to his hut. "Tonight, please let me stay overnight here," she requested. Gombei was very surprised, but he gladly agreed to let her stay.

As night came, the woman said to him, "You are all alone in the world, and so am I; please take me as your wife." Gombei joyfully agreed, and she became his wife.

Gombei was so in love with his new wife that he hardly knew what he was doing. When he would sit down to make straw sandals, he was constantly looking at her, so that sometimes he would make the sandals five or six *shaku* [five or six feet] long, and they would be unfit for anyone to wear. Or when he would start to make straw rain capes, he could not take his eyes off his wife, and the capes would become longer and longer, one or two *jo* [ten to twenty feet], and no one could wear them. Then again, when he would go out to work in the fields, he would begin to wonder if his wife were all right and, after making one furrow, would run home to see her, then return to his work; but he would only get one more furrow made before he would again start thinking about his wife so much that he would have to run home again to see her. In this way he was hardly able to get any work done at all.

Since her husband could not get his work done, the wife went to the village and had an artist paint her portrait. She brought it home and gave it to Gombei, saying, "Here, this is just like me; please take it and hang it on a branch of a mulberry tree near the field. You can look at it as much as you want as you do your work."

Gombei took the picture and hung it near the field, and from then on he would work every day in the field, always looking at the picture. One day, however, a great wind came and, picking up the picture, whirled it high up into the air. Gombei was grief-stricken. Crying bitterly, he returned home to tell his wife what had happened. She comforted him, saying, "Do not worry so about it. I can easily have another painted just like it."

The wind carried the picture about here and there, finally letting it fall in the garden of the lord of the province. When the lord saw the picture, he thought it so beautiful that he greatly desired to marry the woman whose portrait it was. He commanded his retainers, saying, "Since this picture has been painted, this beautiful woman must surely exist somewhere. You must go and find her for me."

The retainers took the picture and went about from village to village, asking everyone they met if they knew where the woman whose portrait it was might be found. Finally they came to the village where Gombei lived. There they asked, "Do you know the woman who is painted here?" The villagers replied, "Yes, that woman is the wife of Gombei." The retainers went to the hut where Gombei lived, and there they found that the woman was exactly like the picture.

"The lord of the province has commanded us to take this woman with us," said the retainers, forcing her to go with them.

"Have mercy on me, please. Please have mercy on me," Gombei pleaded, but to no avail, and his wife was taken away. Gombei, stricken with grief, cried endlessly. His nose began to run. The mucus mixed with his tears and made a stream reaching clear to the ground. His wife too cried and cried. "Gombei," she sobbed, "there is no way out; I must go. But when the end of the year comes, you must come to the lord's castle and sell pine trees for the new year's gate decorations. If you do that, we can surely meet again." Saying this, she was taken away.

Soon the end of the year drew near. Gombei took a large bundle of young pine trees on his back and merrily set off for the lord's castle. When he came to the front gate of the castle, he called out in a loud voice, "Gate pines for sale! Gate pines for sale!"

As soon as she heard Gombei's voice outside, his wife, who until then had never even smiled, broke into merry laughter. The lord was so happy to see her laugh that he ordered his retainers to bring in the man selling pine trees. When Gombei was brought in, the woman again laughed happily.

The lord was overjoyed and said, "If you enjoy the pine tree peddler so much, I shall become one, and you shall be happier than ever." Saying this, he put his own robes on Gombei and took Gombei's dirty rags and put them on. He loaded the pine trees on his back and danced about calling, "Gate pines for sale! Gate pines for sale!"

When she saw this, the woman looked happier than ever before and again burst out in laughter. The lord was so pleased that he went through the gates and outside the castle, walking along calling, "Gate pines for sale! Gate pines for sale!"

As soon as he was gone, the woman ordered the retainers to close the iron gates securely and lock them. After a short while the lord returned. When he found that the gates were shut, he was very surprised. Pounding on the doors of the gate, he called, "The lord is outside, the lord is outside," but no one would open the gates.

Inside the castle, Gombei and his wife, surrounded by many servants, spent the rest of their lives in peace and luxury.

Ichigo buranto kudatta. "The market was good; everything sold out."

from

Letters to a Young Poet

Rainer Maria Rilke

Translated by Stephen Mitchell

Paris

February 17,1903

Dear Sir,

Your letter arrived just a few days ago. I want to thank you for the great confidence you have placed in me. That is all I can do. I cannot discuss your verses; for any attempt at criticism would be foreign to me. Nothing touches a work of art so little as words of criticism: they always result in more or less fortunate misunderstandings. Things aren't all so tangible and sayable as people would usually have us believe; most experiences are unsayable, they happen in a space that no word has ever entered, and more unsayable than all other things are works of art, those mysterious existences, whose life endures beside our own small, transitory life.

With this note as a preface, may I just tell you that your verses have no style of their own, although they do have silent and hidden beginnings of something personal. I feel this most clearly in the last poem, "My Soul." There, something of your own is trying to become word and melody. And in the lovely poem "To Leopardi" a kind of kinship with that great, solitary figure does perhaps appear. Nevertheless, the poems are not yet anything in themselves, not yet anything independent, even the last one and the one to Leopardi. Your kind letter, which accompanied them, managed to make clear to me various faults that I felt in reading your verses, though I am not able to name them specifically.

You ask whether your verses are any good. You ask me. You have asked others before this. You send them to maga- zines. You compare them with other poems, and you are upset when certain editors reject your work. Now (since you have said you want my advice) I beg you to stop doing that sort of thing. You are looking outside, and that is what you should most avoid right now. No one can advise or help you—no one. There is only one thing you should do. Go into yourself. Find out the reason that commands you to write; see whether it has spread its roots into the very depths of your heart; confess to yourself whether you would have to die if you were forbidden to write. This most of all: ask your- self in the most silent hour of your night: *must* I write? Dig into yourself for a deep answer. And if this answer rings out in assent, if you meet this solemn question with a strong, simple *"I must,"* then build your life in accordance with this necessity; your whole life, even into its humblest and most indifferent hour, must become a sign and witness to this impulse. Then come close to Nature. Then, as if no one had ever tried before, try to say what you see and feel and love and lose. Don't write love poems; avoid those forms that are too facile and ordinary: they are the hardest to work with, and it takes a great, fully ripened power to create something individual where good, even glorious, traditions exist in abundance. So rescue yourself from these general themes and write about what your everyday life offers you; describe your sorrows and desires, the thoughts that pass through your mind and your belief in some kind of beauty—describe all these with heartfelt, silent, humble sincerity and, when you express yourself, use the Things around you, the im- ages from your dreams, and the objects that you remember. If your everyday life seems poor, don't blame *it;* blame your- self; admit to yourself that you are not enough of a poet to call forth its riches; because for the creator there is no poverty and no poor, indifferent place. And even if you found yourself in some prison, whose walls let in none of the world's sounds—wouldn't you still have your childhood, that jewel beyond all price, that treasure house of memo- ries? Turn your attention to it. Try to raise up the sunken feelings of this enormous past; your personality will grow stronger, your solitude will expand and become a place where you can live in the twilight, where the noise of other people passes by, far in the distance.—And if out of this turning-within, out of this immersion in your own world, *poems* come, then you will not think of asking anyone whether they are good or not. Nor will you try to interest magazines in these works: for you will see them as your dear natural possession, a piece of your life, a voice from it. A work of art is good if it has arisen out of necessity. That is the only way one can judge it. So, dear Sir, I can't give you any advice but this: to go into yourself and see how deep the place is from which your life flows; at its source you will find the answer to the question of whether you *must* create. Accept that answer, just as it is given to you, without trying to interpret it. Perhaps you will discover that you are called to be an artist. Then take that destiny upon yourself, and bear it, its burden and its greatness, without ever asking what reward might come from outside. For the creator must be a world for himself and must find everything in himself and in Nature, to whom his whole life is devoted. . . .

Acknowledgments *(continued from p. ii)*

Random House, Inc.

From *Letters to a Young Poet* by Rainer Maria Rilke, translated by Stephen Mitchell. Copyright © 1984 by Stephen Mitchell. Reprinted by permission of Random House, Inc.

Time-Life Books, Inc.

From *Time-Life Library of Art: The World of Velázquez, 1599–1660* by Dale Brown and The Editors of Time-Life Books. © 1969 Time-Life Books, Inc. Used by permission of Time-Life Books, Inc.

University of Chicago Press

"The Wife's Portrait" by Keigo Seki (Japan) from *The Folktales of the World Series*, edited by Richard M. Dorson, by permission of the University of Chicago Press.

Note: Every effort has been made to locate the copyright owner of material reprinted in this book. Omissions brought to our attention will be corrected in subsequent editions.